D0897673

N

MUSICAL TERMINOLOGY

A PRACTICAL COMPENDIUM IN FOUR LANGUAGES

MUSICAL TERMINOLOGY

A PRACTICAL COMPENDIUM

IN FOUR LANGUAGES

compiled by

David L. Boccagna

Pendragon Press
Stuyvesant, NY

Pendragon Series in Musicology

Aesthetics in Music

Annotated Reference Tools in Music

Bucina: The Historic Brass Society Series

Croatian Musicological Society Series

Dance & Music

Dimension & Diversity: Studies in 20th-Century Music

The Festschrift Series

The Franz Liszt Studies Series

French Opera in the 17th And 18th Centuries

Harmonologia: Studies in Music Theory

Historical Harpsichord

Interplay: Music in Inter-disciplinary Dialogue

Mannes Studies in Music

Monographs in Musicology

Musical Life in 19th-century France

The Complete Organ

The Complete Works of G. B. Pergolesi

Pergolesi Studies\Studi Pergolesiani

The Polish Music History Series

The Sociology of Music

Studies in Central & Eastern European Music

Studies in Czech Music

Thematic Catalogues

Vox Musicae

Library of Congress Cataloging-in-Publication Data

Musical Terminology: a practical compendium in four languages / compiled by David L. Boccagna

p. cm.

In Italian, English, French, and German.

Includes bibliographical references.

ISBN 1-57647-015-6

1. Music—Performance Terminology.

ML 108.B55   1999

780'.3—dc21

99-31743

CIP

Table of Contents

Acknowledgments

Among the large number of individuals who have contributed to the compilation of this compendium I wish to give special recognition to the following, who provided the inspiration I could not do without: Julius Baker, Edward Hall Broadhead, Joseph Iadone, John Mahoney, Ferdinand A. Pasqua, and Gustave Reese.

I would also like to extend a very special thanks to Kaz, Kim, and Kai to whom I am most grateful.

David L. Boccagna, PhD.

CHAPTER I

INTRODUCTION

This compendium of agogic[1] terms is the result of many years of compiling, organizing, editing, and formulating the words and phrases into an intelligible and handy tool for use by my students and myself. Its need was made manifest more than fifteen years ago when students playing foreign music editions would ask what specific terms meant and what their equivalents were in English. I, too, found myself repeatedly consulting various musical sources for the specific meanings of terms that I did not know or definitions I had forgotten. At first these terms, written on slips of paper, were filed in a folder. As these slips began to accumulate, it took as long to sift through the folder as it took to find a particular definition in a music dictionary. Organizing these terms on sheets of paper according to language proved to be of limited value as their number grew so rapidly that they had to be alphabetized. The convenience of the alphabet afforded one the opportunity of checking, by cross-reference, other related terms in the same as well as in different languages. This, in fact, paved the way for the next phase in the development of the compendium. Each term was alphabetized by language in the left hand column and immediately following it in separate columns

[1]The term *Agogic* was first introduced by Hugo Riemann in his treatise *Musikalische Dynamik und Agogik* in 1884. It was intended to describe deviations from strict tempo and rhythm.

were the term's equivalents in the three other most commonly used languages. Eventually it became obvious that not all the terms were directly translatable into the other languages—especially as it pertained to musical equivalents. It was then decided that, in those cases, the closest possible synonym was found and placed in the adjacent language columns. In all cases, the synonyms selected are of musical origin, and not just arbitrarily selected words with similar meanings.

After much deliberation, it seemed advisable to include the ordinary words in any of the languages—the equivalents of "the," "of," "to," etc.—since they were often combined with musical terms to achieve a strictly musical instruction (as for example, "a tempo" or "da capo.")

All of the definitions in this compendium have been checked in the *Harvard Dictionary of Music, Baker's Dictionary of Musical Terms, Elson's Dictionary of Musical Terms, The Oxford Companion to Music*, and *Terminorum Musicae Index Septem Linguis Redactuis*. Some were further checked in *Grove's Dictionary of Music and Musicians*, sixth edition. The terms themselves were selected not only for their importance to today's musicians, but also because they appear most frequently in printed music most commonly used by performers. The decisive factors in determining which terms were to be included were: frequency with which a term appeared in contemporary music and frequency with which it appeared during each specific historic musical period. Those terms which are peculiar to a specific instrument, such as *col legno* (with the wood of the bow against the string) or *registration* (combining organ registers) have not been included. Terms with multiple definitions that have changed over the years appear with the one definition that has been retained. However, when those former definitions are still significant today, they too have been included. The definition of every term in this compendium, whether English, French, German, or Italian, had to appear in at least two of the sources listed above in order to be included in this volume. The spellings as well as the definitions found in those sources were also checked in the *Cassells, Garzanti, Langenscheidt*, and *Palazzi* dictionaries.[2]

A bank of terms of English definitions was added once the French, German and Italian sections were completed. This section contains all of the terms that appear in the other sections. Here the English definition that appeared most frequently in the other sources is the one included in the compendium. This section serves two very important purposes:

---

[2]Reference may be made to any edition of the following, but the ones found in this study are:

The New Cassell's French Dictionary. Completely revised by Denis Girard (New York, 1962).

The New Cassell's German Dictionary. Based on the editions by Karl Breul, completely revised by Harold T. Betteridge (New York, 1971).

Cassel's Italian Dictionary. Compiled by Piero Rebora (New York, 1967).

Garzanti Comprehensive Italian English Dictionary. Edited by Mario Hazon (New York, 1961).

Palazzi Novissimo Dizionario Della Lingua Italiana (Milano, 1939).

Langenscheidt's German-English Dictionary. Edited by the Langenscheidt Editorial Staff (New York, 1970).

1) as a source for composers who can now describe a mood or setting more accurately by selecting a term from the compendium rather than settling for the only definition they might know; 2) as a further aid to the English-, French-, German-, and Italian-speaking instrumentalists who can now check a term's equivalents in the three other languages to better understand what the composer intended. The arrangement of the materials in four separate alphabets facilitates user-access by accomodating the language with which the user is familiar.

HOW THE COMPENDIUM IS ORGANIZED

This compendium is divided into four sections (reading from left to right):

Section one:

ITALIAN—FRENCH—GERMAN—ENGLISH

Section two:

FRENCH—GERMAN—ITALIAN—ENGLISH

Section three:

GERMAN—ITALIAN—FRENCH—ENGLISH

Section four:

ENGLISH—ITALIAN—FRENCH—GERMAN

Each pair of facing pages is divided into four columns. Every word, phrase, or agogic term that appears in the first (left-hand) column of each foreign language section will have its English translation in the fourth (far right-hand) column. In the second and third columns the word, phrase, or term's equivalents in the two other languages will appear. Because many words are not directly translatable into another language, additional synonyms appear in each language column. It is therefore suggested that when a word's equivalent is being sought in another language, the user look up the synonym in English. For example: if one were looking for a word in Italian meaning "dying away," refer to the English section first; after finding "dying away," look in the adjacent column containing the Italian equivalents and synonyms. One would then discover that *morendo, mancando, sperdendosi, diminuendo, scemando* all translate into "dying away" in English. One would also discover that the French equivalents are *diminuer, eteindre,* and *en mourant*; in German, one could say *leiser werdend, hinsterbend,* or *verhallend.*

CHAPTER II

THE EVOLUTION OF AGOGIC TERMS

A certain ambiguity in musical terms is not only necessary but desirable. Terms such as *Lento, Adagio, Andante, Allegro, Presto* not only describe degrees of speed, but they also refer to the character of a piece. The slow movement of a symphony is frequently referred to as "the" *Adagio*, but the term has a wider meaning. It must fit descriptively into a particular mood in order to be an *Adagio* and not an *Andante*, for example. That intangible something is as hard to pin down as it is to describe color to a blind person who has never seen any.

There have been many factors influencing the evolution of agogic[3] terms as well as their particular usage:

> The history of early devices
> The invention of the stave
> Instrumental music
> Development of new styles of performance and
> > composition
> Invention of new instruments and improvement of
> > the old
> New musical forms, especially opera and the overture
> Need for new expressive terminology
> The influence of the Mannheim School

---

[3]See footnote 1; however, here "agogic" denotes all of the subtleties of performance—those which fall under the category of modification of tempo as well as those relating to the subtleties of performance.

THE HISTORY OF EARLY DEVICES

Musical terms are instructions or directions to the performing musician that serve as an aid to the interpretation of the musical symbols—the notes and rests appearing on a stave. The earliest device used, in addition to the neumes,[4] was *musica ficta*, the accidentals inserted or implied in a score to avoid the "diabolus in musica."[5]

The *Melodic Musica Ficta*[6] appears below between the following signs:

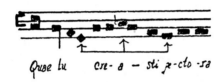

Quse lu cre- a — sti p-cto -sa

---

[4] Neumes were notational signs used in the Middle Ages that were applicable to single tones as well as groups of tones. For example, the *Punctum* ■ represented one note and the *Porrectus flexus*, ◣■ four notes. These notational signs stood for approximate pitch only and rhythm was determined by the text. Originally, neumes were mnemonic devices for singers who already knew the melodies they were singing and served primarily as visual aids to depict the rise and fall of those familiar melodies.

[5] The "diabolus in musica" was the medieval term for the interval of an augmented fourth or diminished fifth (tri-tone) in composition. This interval was to be avoided melodically and also where two polyphonic voices came together to form the tri-tone. In Medieval and Renaissance music, the accidentals were understood in applicable contexts so were not written out. Modern performers need to have them added, but it is not always clear where.

[6] Dom Anselm Hughes, *Early Medieval Music up to 1300* (New York, 1955), p. 371.

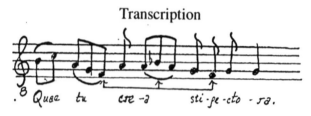

The *Harmonic Musica Ficta*[7] is designated below by a double arrow:

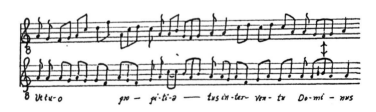

Transcription

---

[7]Ibid, p. 308.

nos par·ga·tos a pec·ca·tis jun·gat coe-li' ci - vi — bus.

Composers from the earliest times have supplied occasional guides and modifications for the performance of their music. These words of wisdom and even the accidental signs which composers inserted throughout a piece were direct reflections on the competence of the performer and were known as *signum asinimum* or "asses' mark."[8] Although from these earliest times there was no unanimity or uniformity of rules set in practice, the theories were undoubtedly evolved long after a performing practice was established. One may wonder if any single practice was in fact "the way it was done" or was it something created after the fact in the mind of the theorist.

THE INVENTION OF THE STAVE

One theorist, Guido d'Arezzo (c. 991-after 1033), did put a system in writing, set down in his famous work, the *Micrologus*[9] (c. 1025). Guido designated the six tones of the

---

[8]Origin debated.
[9]Guido, in his *Prologus Antiphonarii sui* (c. 1025), suggested the use of three, four, and five lines to a stave. However, since the stave was in existence much before his time, he was not its inventor. Guido suggested coloring lines of the stave to aid the singer in identifying the lines by name and also in fixing relative pitches of C and F (and sometimes B♭). (cont.)

10

hexachord by the vocables ut, re, mi, fa, sol, la. The melody of the *Hymn to St. John the Baptist* has the characteristic of beginning one tone higher on each successive line.

Hymn to St. John the Baptist[10]

The *Hymn to St. John the Baptist* and its designated tones (ut, re, mi, fa, sol, la) were placed on the existing stave and served as a mnemonic device to help the singer remember where certain notes and pitches were—in other words, a definite notation was thus produced. In the prologue to the *Micrologus*, Guido wrote of the results of singing from specific notation: "Some of the boys, who had practiced intervals from the monochord and from our notation, were able in less than a month to sing at first sight and without hesitation chants which they had previously never seen or heard."
[10]Dom Anselm Huighes, *Op cit.*, p. 291.

Labii re — o-tum, Son — cte Jo — an — nes.

> *Ut* queant laxis
> *Re*sonare fibris
> *Mi*ra gestorum
> *Fa*muli tuorum
> *Sol*ve polluti
> *La*bia reatum
> *Sa*ncte *Johannes.*

(That with relaxed (vocal) chords thy servants may be able to sing the wonders of thy deeds, remove the sin from their polluted lips, O Holy John.)[11]

The "Guidonian Hand"[12] was a device to aid teachers in understanding the hexachord, solmization, and imitation. To capsulize the above, it became a method of movable Do.

The sketch below served to help memorize the scale and its solmization syllables.

---

[11]Willi Apel, *Harvard Dictionary of Music* (Cambridge, MA: Harvard University Press, 1962) p. 331.

[12]The so-called Guidonian hand is not treated in any of Guido's surviving works but is found drawn or mentioned in the following old documents: Charles Edmund Coussemaker, *Scriptorum de musica medii aevi nova series* (Milan, 1931); John Hawkins, *A General History of the Science and Practice of Music* (London, 1875).

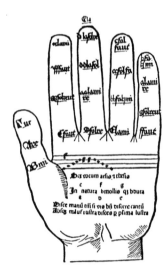

Neumatic notation represented phrasing groups and the general curve of the chant. Guido's method was to draw a yellow line for C, a red line for F, and a green line if B♭ were needed. The remaining lines were drawn in black and the principal of the stave was established.

From the early times of polyphony, especially during the twelfth and thirteenth centuries, the mechanics of notation were in a continuous state of flux and were usually governed by the rhythm that was, in turn, dictated by the text. One of the difficulties encountered was keeping the voices together at key points in the melody. As early as the twelfth century, a specific method for achieving this is not easily identified. Interpretation of the notational schemes used by scribes is extremely precarious as there are numerous "modern" scholarly methods or approaches possible. Positive conclusions are, at best, doubtful. The problems of polyphonic vocal notation were probably not as complex to the performer then as they appear to be to today's interpretors of yesterdays' music.[13]

INSTRUMENTAL MUSIC

With the advent of instrumental part music (c. 1500)[14] the problems confronting the medieval scribes grew. Having the pholyphonic voices landing together at key points now was critical at every beat in every measure. Observe the lines drawn in the manuscript below that were used to keep the voices together:

---

[13]Willi Apel, *The Notation of Polyphonic Music*, 900-1600 (Cambridge, Mass, 1944).
[14]Mensurable notation is the term that refers to strictly measurable and unambiguous notational characters both black (1250-1450) and white (1450-1600) that were used for the notation of ensemble or instrumental music. Although mensurable notation, both black and white, is complicated, it was adequate and provided the accuracy for (cont.) notating precisely the pitch and rhythm that was most definitely needed for instrumental part music.

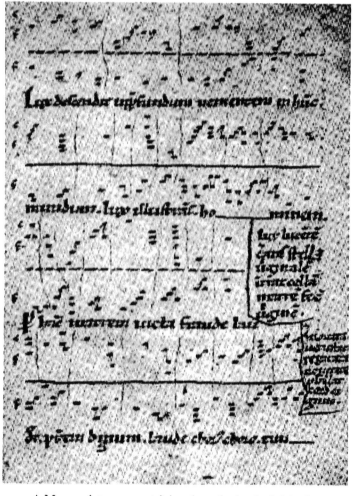

A Manuscript page containing the polyphonic St.Martial
organum, *Lux descendit*.[15]

[15]Donald J. Grout, *A History of Western Music* (New York, 1960), p. 72.

The problem of notating pitch and rhythm was now sufficiently advanced to warrant additional symbols and devices in order to instruct the instrumentalist in the skills of interpretation.

Interesting observations can be made from the following words of the twelfth-century Bishop Aeldred. Each letter in brackets immediately after a phrase is explained below the text.

To what purpose serves that contraction (a) and inflection (b) of the voyce? This man sings base, that a small meane, another a treble, a fourth divides and cuts asunder, as it were, certaine middle notes. One while the voyce is strained, anon it is remitted, now it is dashed, and then againe it is enlarged with a lowder sound. Sometimes, which is a shame to speake, it is enforced into a horse's neighings (c) sometimes, the masculine vigour being laid aside (d), it is sharpened into the shrilnesse of a woman's voyce; now and then it is writhed, and retorted with a certaine articifical circumvolution (e). Sometimes thou may'st see a man with a open mouth (f), not to sing, but, as it were, to breathe out his last gaspe, by shutting in his breath, and by certaine ridiculous interception of his voyce, as it were to threaten silence, and now againe to imitate the agonies of adying man, or the extasies of such as suffer.[16]

    (a) Diminuendo
    (b) Crescendo

[16]Eric Bloom, ed., *Grove's Dictionary of Music and Musicians,* (London, 1954), p. 367, Vol. VI, taken from the translation of Wm. Prynne *Histriomastix; the players' scourge*, chapter XX (1633).

    (c) Tremolo

    (d) Falsetto

    (e) Trill or Shake

    (f) Hocket

During the Baroque Period, we have symbols representing the many possible ornamentations. Specific names are now given to each ornament and a list of signs along with instructions as to how they are to be interpreted or executed.

The following chart was taken from a table which appeared in the fourth edition of *Grove's Dictionary*, pp. 441-48. Numbers 3, 8, 12, 20, 25, 54, 87, and 96 listed below were randomly selected from the table's 125 ornaments[17] as examples.

No.	Sign	Ornament	Rough Guide to Use or Source
3.	.˙.	Single relish (virtually a brief trill with a turned ending).	Mace (but also used in 17th century England as a repeat sign)
8.	▼	a) Curtailed note b) Staccato more generally	a) Couperin, Rameau b) General 18th century

---

[17]Additional insight can be obtained from the following references. Each one is an important source on the interpretation of embellishments: Carl Philip Emanuel Bach, *Essay on the True Art of playing Keyboard Instruments* (New York, 1949); Leopold Mozart, *A Treatise on the Fundamental Principles of Violin Playing* (London, 1951); Joachim Quantz, *Essay on the Method of Playing the Transverse Flute* (New York, 1966).

No.	Sign	Ornament	Rough Guide to Use or Source
12.	⚹	Rising stroke through stem if there is one: a) Mordent b) Half-shake c) ?Trill d) Ascending slide	English virginalists (late 16th to early 17th centuries) (Use not entirely certain)
20.	/	Before note: a) Lower appoggiatura b) Ascending slide c) Rising note of anticipation or similar Nachschlag	a) Widely current 17th century to mid-18th century. England, Italy, Germany.) b) Chiefly French, same dates; also given by Turk. c) Later 18th Century German
25.	\	Before note: a) Falling note of anticipation b) Upper appoggiatura c) Descending slide.	a) 17th century English including Purcell; also Turk. b) J.G. Walther; Th. Muffat. c) Turk.
54.	⌁⌁⌁	a) Trill b) Double mordent c) Appoggiatura-prepared lower mordent. d) Prepared trill e) Ascending trill. f) Vibrato g) Tremolo.	a) Ubiquitous French and German from 17th century: the correct usage. b) Loulie. c) ? Locke, Purcell. d) L'Affilard. e) Th. Muffat. f) Mace. g) L'Affilard.
87.	∿	a) Turn b) Inverted turn	a) English, French, German; the ubiquitous sign from 17th century to present day: the correct usage.

No.	Sign	Ornament	Rough Guide to Use or Source
96.	❟	Comma after note: a) Trill b) Lower appoggiatura c) Mordent	a) French 17th and 18th centuries: the main usage. b) French 17th and 18th century lutenists. c) French 17th and 18th century.

These signs and terms were inherited by Baroque musicians from their predecessors. Only now instead of the melodic importance these signs had in Renaissance music, new harmonic significance is given the same embellishments by the Baroque composers and virtuosi.

DEVELOPMENT OF NEW STYLES OF PERFORMANCE AND COMPOSITION

With the coming of the Baroque period at the turn of the seventeenth century, many composers began to develop a specific style of composition and performance. Emotional appeal to the listeners' hearts was important. Italian singers expressed passions so violently that the audience would think itself involved. It is purported that in one of Monteverdi's operas, performed in 1608 at the Mantuan court, Arianna, forsaken by Theseus, sang her heart-rending lament and the audience burst into tears.

The new approaches to singing and performance demanded sudden changes from joy to grief and from melancholy to exultation. For the first time, we begin to find directions and specific instructions for singers and instrumentalists. This new style initially manifested itself in vocal music, but soon asserted itself in instrumental music as well. In 1613, Salomone Rossi (1570-1630) wrote the first sonata for two violins and in 1617, Biagio Marini (1587-1663) wrote the first sonata for one violin. Both were in the *stile rappresentativo*[18] to be performed in a manner demonstrating a high, emotional style.

INVENTION OF NEW INSTRUMENTS AND IMPROVEMENT OF THE OLD

Instruments were now beginning to undergo a process of severe change. Those capable of extreme flexibility in duplicating the human voice with all of its inherent qualities, especially the dynamic shades from pianissimo to fortissimo, were now the instruments of choice. Those not capable of offering a wide dynamic range, such as cromornes, bagpipes, and schryari, were quickly discarded. The need for contrasts in color and dynamics, as well as attacks of notes and articulations, made greater demands upon the instrumentalists as well as their instruments; in other words, the specific use of agogic terms to describe these changes, became a practical necessity.

---

[18]*Stile Rappresentative*: A type of performance developed around 1600 which is characterized by its reactions against polyphonic music. It was a new style in which speech was imitated as closely as possible. i.e., speech-like reiteration of the same note, slight inflections, short groups of quick notes in irregular rhythms. See: Monteverdi (*Scherzi musicali*, 1607): "*L'orazione sia padrona del' armonia e non s erva*" (The text should be the master and not the servant).

The strings (violin, viola, 'cello, and bass) changed in shape and construction appreciably from their ancestors, the viols. These changes were made to accommodate the technical demands which the music made on the players for technical proficiency as well as the timbre demands upon the string section. The bow also went through changes and it was François Tourte (1747-1835) who finally gave it its modern form. The first evidence of mutes added to the string section appeared in Lully's opera, *Armide* (1686) "*Il faut jouer avec des sourdines.*" In Sylvestro di Ganassi's *Lettione Seconda* (1543) we have the first references to pizzicato and vibrato.

While the strings dominated the Baroque orchestra, some of the woodwinds were undergoing physical changes. These changes were being made to make the winds more coloristically compatible with the strings and also to enhance their cantability and agility. The flute changed the most dramatically of all. It was now played transverse and its tubular dimensions were changed. An extremely important treatise was written in 1752 by Joachim Quantz (see footnote 17); it covered not only the playing of the flute but the interpretation of Baroque music as well. The oboe went through numerous metamorphoses and timbre differentiation was made in 1720 for the first time in George Philip Telemann's opera, *Der Sieg der Schonheit*. This score called for an oboe d'amore, which was a slightly larger instrument than the oboe and of an obviously different tonal color. It is actually similar to the English Horn of today.

The clarinet, as we know it, was not yet invented; it evolved from the folk shawm to an oboe-like instrument created by Johann Christoph Denner (1655-1707) at the end of the seventeenth century. Its subsequent physical changes, brought about by Denner's son Jacob gave it a warmer sound (*chaleureux*) than the oboe. Specific reference was made to its use in the opera *Croesus* (1711) by Reinhard Keiser (1674-1739).

The piano, which went through many modifications before it eventually became the instrument we know today, was invented because the coloristic range of the harpsichord was too limited. Bartolomeo Cristofori (1655-1731)[19] named the earliest pianos "*gravicembalo col pian e forte*" or "harpsichord with the ability to produce piano and forte (by touch)."

Changes in instruments were invariably made to enhance the performers' musicality—a musicality indicated through the use of a descriptive term.

The interchangeability of string and wind parts that had characterized orchestral instrumentation was becoming passé by the beginning of the eighteenth century. A particular part was written to be played by a particular instrument; in fact, the music was actually conceived and orchestrated for that particular instrument. As a result of this "new" approach, agogic terms were appearing more and more frequently in scores and in individual parts directing the players to employ nuances indigenous to their instruments.

[19]Inventor of the piano according to Curt Sachs, *The History of Musical Instruments* (New York, 1940).

The number of characteristic timbres increased at an astonishing rate and the tendency toward expressive emotional music became manifest. General but limited moods of majesty, liveliness, joy, and affliction were now expanded. Composers tried to express all the shadings of human feeling. From the beginning of what we call the Romantic period (c. 1820), little discretion was left to the performer. The composer's demands were precise and orchestration became an independant aspect of musical composition. The performer had to learn a new terminology, whose interpretation and subsequent application coincided with the composer's intentions. In all cases, emotion was the principal requirement. Instruments had gone through sufficient changes and innovation, and were finally flexible enough to permit the players to work within the full gamut of available possibilities. They could also span the full range of emotions called for by the agogic terms. This marvelous stage in the development and usage of these descriptive terms became even more astounding when they were applied to opera.

THE OPERA AND OVERTURE

One of the larger forms that emerged during the Baroque period was opera. An opera usually began with an overture, i.e. an instrumental prelude. Monteverdi's *Orfeo* (1607) opened with an instrumental flourish of just nine measures; however, Lully, in his operas and ballets, dating from 1672 to 1686, included an overture in each. The basic tempo differences between the French and Italian overtures were simple:

the French overture began with a slow section and the Italian overture with a fast one. The common pattern of the French overture was slow, fast, slow and the Italian overture fast, slow, fast. These tempos, of course, required the labeling of such movements as Adagio, Allegro, Andante for the French or Presto, Andante, Allegro for the Italian. Here the musical terms refer to character as well as tempo or speed. However, a term was now incorporated in the descriptive instructions—another innovation in the use of agogic terms.

As opera developed, new terms were added. The ballets, choruses, short simple songs, mostly of a dance-like character, elaborate arias, and the important parts given to the orchestra, had to compliment the lengthy vocalizations. Many concertizing instrumentations were utilized to enhance the vocal solos. All of this was in addition to the full range of opera types (viz., *opera buffa, opera seria*, classical tragedy, drama, pompousness, majesty, melodrama), different types of arias (*aria cantabiule, aria parlante, aria di bravura*) new vocal techniques (*bel canto*) and the uniqueness of the *Castrati*—all of these facets had to be coordinated with the music. Another basic characteristic of opera is that it usually takes longer for the musical development of an idea than it would require merely to speak the words with which it is linked. This results in one of more of the following: a stretching out and consequent slowing of the pace of the action; or alternating periods of action and repose (i.e. the action being carried on through recitative interrupted by arias, ensembles or ballets). All of these facets had to be signalled to the performing musicians through descriptive phrases and agogic terms. This became a language to aid and extend the understanding of the music symbols on the page conceived by the composer in a union of music, verse, action, costumes, scenery, and drama.

NEED FOR NEW EXPRESSIVE TERMINOLOGY

Our present system of musical notation can prescribe precisely what is to be played; however, it can only hint, and very vaguely at best, at how it is to be played. To aid the performer in the "how," descriptive terms are employed. These terms are used far more frequently today than formerly but this still does not enable today's performers to play any more expressively than their predecessors. Actually, the limitation is inherent in musical notation, but expression, or the "how" on the other hand, is unlimited in the many graduations of intensity that are possible within performance expressiveness.

All of the nuances of *tempo, dynamics, accent, attack, phrasing*, etc., offer the performer more freedom than the mere playing of notes. In music prior to 1600 there were no directions given to the performer. At that time great latitude was granted in the expressive aspects of the art. However, gradually composers felt the need to be more specific in their instructions. They sought to limit the performer by clarifying their intentions, to prevent mistakes, and more specifically, to curtail a kind of emotional wandering far afield. This led to the gradual introduction of tempo indications, dynamic marks, and descriptive terms that testified to the general character of the composition.

The mood, character, or setting of a composition was most important. These were indicated by descriptive words at the beginning of the work. In music prior to 1600, indications such as *Allegro, Andante,* etc. were not necessary because the tempo of a piece was clearly expressed by its notation. The tempo was realized through its *tactus* (the fifteenth and sixteenth century term for beat). The *tactus* was a relatively fixed duration of time of about one per second (metronome marking about 60). Music of the Flemish Schools, therefore, was within a given or fixed tempo allowing for very little if any variation.[20]

Perhaps the inclusion of descriptive terms at the beginning of a piece to give some broad indication of its mood and character might be traced to dance music. The dance forms found collected in the suite, such as the Pavan, Galliard, Saraband, Gigue, etc., each had its own dance steps fitted into a certain tempo or rhythmic mood.

The written indications of tempo as specified in Luis de Milan's music became more and more frequent in seventeenth-century composition. Problems arose later in the eighteenth century—problems which still exist today—as to what

[20]The earliest instance of the variability of tempo appears in Luis de Milan's (c.1500-1561) lute book *El Maestro* 1535). Here he asks that certain passages are to be played, "*a priesa*" (quick) and for others "*a espacio*" (slow). Adriano Banchieri (1568-1634) is reported as the first (c.1600) to use such tempo indications as *Allegro, Adagio*, and *Presto*.

specifically is meant by each of those terms. Brossard[21] in 1703 described the French minuet as "very gay and fast" but Diderot[22] in 1751 described the same dance as "noble and elegant, moderate rather than quick." In 1733, Grassineau[23] described presto as "fast or quick, gayly yet not with rapidity" and C. P. E. Bach in his famous treatise of 1753 wrote:

> The speed of a work, which is usually suggested by various familiar Italian terms, depends upon its general character and also on the speed of the fastest notes and passage-work which it contains. Proper attention to these considerations will prevent an allegro from being hurried and an adagio from being dragged.[24]

The musical terms which appear at the beginning of a composition do not indicate pace or tempo only. The character, the mood, or the scene being described are far more important than the speed of a piece. Before a performer can decide how fast a piece is to be played, the mood or character must be determined; then, relating pace to mood, the tempo that best fits the character made manifest in the composition will be chosen; also, it must be decided whether the character will be clearly demonstrable by the speed selected. Within this framework of fitting character and complimentary tempo, the artist-performer has the option of varying the established pace. Some of the words which indicate these fluctuations are

[21]Sebastien de Brossard, *Dictionnaire de musique* (Amsterdam, 1709).
[22]Denis Diderot, *Encyclopédie ou dictionnaire raisonné des sciences, des arts* (Paris, 1751).
[23] J. Grassineau, *A Musical Dictionary-Carefully abstracted from the Best Authors* (London, 1740).
[24]Carl Philip Emanuel Bach, *Op. cit.*

Ritardando, Accelerando, Più mosso, Rallentando, etc. At other points the artist-performer may make additional aesthetic variations.

Much has been written about expressive fluctuations, which may be categorized as the following: (1) fluctuations which occur by borrowing time from one note and giving to another all within the same measure—thus, the established temporal duration is not disturbed but only the notes within the measure; (2) fluctuations which extend beyond the measure line and redefine the established rhythm.

In reference to the fluctuations in the first category, Couperin stated "the spirit, the soul that must be added to the mere quantity and quality of beats is that which makes up these fluctuations."[25] Rousseau wrote "... one can play in time without entering into the movement, because the time depends only on the music, but the movement depends on genius and good taste."[26]

With regard to the second category, the *Ritardando* and *Accelerando* are mentioned frequently by seventeenth- and eighteenth-century composers. Frescobaldi stated "the cadences, though written rapid, are to be played in a very sustained manner; the nearer you approach the cadence, the nearer you should hold back the tempo."[27] Mace suggested

[25]François Couperin, *L'Art de toucher le clavecin* (Paris, 1717).
[26]Jean-Jacques Rousseau *Dictionnaire de musique* (Paris, 1768).
[27]Girolamo Frescobaldi, *Toccatas of 1614* (New York, 1950).

"Liberty to break time; sometimes faster and sometimes lower, as we perceive the nature of the thing requires."[28]

Although tempo fluctuations are not directly related to rhythmical changes, they do affect the liveliness of the music. Rhythm is related to accentuation and, of course, to the type of stress or accent being used. Of all the descriptive terms usually employed, *marcato* is the most qeneral indication of accentuation, bearing on the dynamic level of attack, the duration of the note being attacked, the intensity of the note being attacked, or the force applied to the note, i.e., at the instant of attack or immediately after. *Sforzando*, another aspect of accentuation, is effected by a slightly more gradual increase of volume occuring imediately after the start of the note.

Dynamic level, in turn, is very closely related to accentuation, i.e., the loud and soft levels which change continually thoughout a composition. By the end of the seventeenth century, the Italian terms *forte* and *piano* had become universal. Their abbreviations *f, ff, p,* and *pp* have also been extensively used.

Changes in volume from *crescendo* to *decrescendo* originated in the Mannheim School, and by the end of the eighteenth century these dynamic changes were being practiced by the leading singers and instrumentalists.[29]

---

[28]Thomas Mace, *Music's Monument* (London, 1676).
[29]Giulio Caccini, *Nuove musiche* (Venice, 1615).

Quantz, in his treatise on the playing of the flute,[30] suggested that the players "increase or diminish the tone when required," and Geminiani[31] and Rameau[32] used signs similar to those used today for *Crescendo* and *Decrescendo* .

"Expression" was certainly present in early music; however, it was not notated in the score. The informed player closely followed the rise and fall of the melody. Special signs were not needed because the very small graduations of intensity that reflected the melody's contour were inherent to it. In about 1600 indications for *forte* and *piano* were introduced in the music, since the styles of performance which emanated from this period, especially the echo[33], *Stile concertato,*[34] and *Stile concitato*[35] required them.

The earliest pieces extant which contained such indications were Giovanni Gabrieli's (c.1553-1612) "Sonata pian' e forte" (c. 1600) and a few organ pieces from 1600 by Adriano Banchieri. In 1638 Domenico Mazzochi stated in his "Partitura de Madrigali ..." that the letters F. P. E. (for *forte*, *piano*, and echo) were already known to all musicians and

---

[30]Joachim Quantz, *Op. cit.* (New York, 1966).

[31]Francesco Geminiani, *The Art of Playing on the Violin* (New York, 1952).

[32]G. Girdlestone, *Jean-Phillipe Rameau, His Life and Work* (London, 1957).

[33]Echo: the statement of a musical phrase *forte* and immediately restated in *piano*.

[34]*Stile concertato*: Seventeenth-century treatment of one section against another in a concerto-like manner displaying bravura and virtuoso characteristics.

[35]*Stile concitato*: The "agitated" style of dramatic expression in instrumental performance used by Claudio Monteverdi.

therefore considered common knowledge. Mazzochi also appeared to be the first to indicate *Crescendo* and *Decrescendo*, the former with a *V* and the latter by a *C* (actually the *C* represented a *Crescendo* followed by a *Dimuendo*). In 1676, Mace, in his *Musick's Monument,* indicated dynamic contrast by *Lo* (loud) and *So* (soft). The modern manner of incorporating all of these signs was cultivated by the members of the Mannheim School. It was here, in Mannheim, Germany, that dynamic effects were developed for the purpose of orchestral coloring as well for climactic effects.

THE INFLUENCE OF THE MANNHEIM SCHOOL

During the reign of Elector of Palatinate Carl Theodore,[36] the group of musicians who made up the court orchestra were referred to as the Mannheim School. They were not composers but conductors and performers, especially violinists. The founder of this school was, however, a composer, Johann Wenzel Stamitz (1717-1757). Some of the characteristics associated with the Mannheim School were: perfect team-work, fiery and expressive execution, uniform bowing, exciting dynamic effects, accuracy in phrasing in orchestral performance, melodic prominance of the violins, harmonic writing as opposed to contrapuntal, no imitation or fugal style writing, presto character of quick movements, long and extended crescendo and decrescendo devices, unexpected fortes

---

[36]Elector of the Palatinate of Mannheim, Germany, Carl Theodor (1742-1778).

and fortissimos, general rests, broken chords, orchestral effects of tremolo, fully written out orchestral parts and the abandonment of thorough-bass. Burney,[37] in 1772, called the orchestra "an army of generals equally fit to plan a battle as to fight it." Stamitz was the first composer to establish the Allegro - Andante - Minuet Presto sequence in the symphony and gave important and conspicuous tasks to the wind instruments.

One can easily see that in order to have an orchestra with all of the attributes of the Mannheim School, much instruction and direction would have been necessary. The use of agogic terms would undoubtedly have helped make the orchestra function as efficiently as it did.

These terms and phrases were inserted in the score and parts to enable the orchestra to accomplish the effects for which they were so renowned. Expressive symbols such as (*ff*) *fortissimo* and (*pp*) *pianissimo*, long *Crescendos* and *Decrescendos* frequently appeared in the music. Although these devices were exploited by this school and sometimes their use was not necessarily justified by the music, a complete merging of composition and expression were reached in the music of Haydn, Mozart, Beethoven and Schubert. During the Romantic period that followed the possibilities of expression were exploited to the fullest extent. Composers invented an enormous number of devices, terms, expressions, and phrases to describe these new possibilities of subtle expres-

---

[37]Charles Burney, *General History of Music* (London, 1775).

sion. Although the innovations were numerous, one must realize that for each descriptive term there were a multitude of possibilities upon which the performer could draw. Therefore, terms designed to aid can also confuse or obscure the composer's intentions unless there is a common musical understanding shared by both composer and performer.

It is with the intent to further that understanding that this compendium was compiled: to broaden the ground shared by the composer and performer by making available additional synonyms from which the composer could select suitable language and also to which the performer could refer.

ITALIAN

ITALIAN	FRENCH
a due	à deux
a libito, beneplacito	à volanté
a tempo	en measure
abbandonare	lâcher
abbassare, bemollizzare	baisser
abbassare	abaisser
abbellimenti	ornements
abbellimenti vocali	broderies
abbozzo	détente
abilità	dexterité
accentato	accentué, appuyé
acceso, focoso	acceso, avec fouque
accompagnare	accompagner
accordare	accorder
accordo	accord
acustica	acoustique
adagietto	adagietto
addensare, ispessire	augmenter
addolorato	douleur, douloureaux
adirato	colèrique
affannato	angoissé
agitato	animé, agité
al	à
allargare	élargir

GERMAN	ENGLISH
zwei Gesang	two voices or instruments
ad libitum, belieben	freely
im Tact, im Zeitmas	in tempo
loslassen	release (to)
erniedrigen	lower, flatten
niederdrücken	depress (to)
Manieren	ornaments
Singmanieren	vocal ornaments
Entwurf	draft, sketch
Fertigkeit	dexterity
betont	accented, stressed
faurig	fiery
begleiten	accompany (to)
einstimmen	tune (to)
akkord	chord
Akustik	acoustics, science of sound
adagietto	adagietto, faster than adagio
anschwellen	grow louder
betrübt, schmerz	grief, sadness
zornig, erregt	angered, irate
ängstlich	anguished
bewegt	animated
bis	to
erweitern	expand, extend

ITALIAN	*FRENCH*
alternando	changeant [en]
altezza	hauteur
altezza del suono	hauteur du son
alto, acuto	haut, aigu
alzare	hausser
ampio	rond, plein
anacrusi	anacrouse
ancia	anche
andante	andante, allant
animato	animé
animoso, animosamente	animé, hardiment
appassionato	passionné
arco in giu	tiré
arco in su	poussé
ardito, arditamente	audacieux, hardi
armonico	harmonique
armonioso	sonore
arpeggiando, arpeggiato	arpégé
arresto	arrêt, silence
articolare	articuler
articolazione	phrasé
ascoltare	écouter
aspramente	aigrement, âpre
assai	beaucoup, très

GERMAN	ENGLISH
abwechselnd	alternating
Höhe	upper notes, treble
Tonhöhe	pitch, pitch level
hoch	high
erhöhen	raise (to), sharpen
rund	rounded, rich
Auftakt	upbeat
Rohrblatt	reed
andante, gehend	walking , moderately
belebt	brisk, animated
animoso,beherzt	spirited, resolutely
leidenschaftlich	passionately
Herstrich	down bow
Hinstrich	up bow
kühn, keck	bold, courageous
Oberton	overtone
klangvoll	harmonious
arpeggiert, gebrochen	broken, arpeggiated
Stillstand	stop
absetzen	separate (t0), articulate (to)
Phrasieruing	phrasing
zuhören	listen (to)
rauh, hart-klingend	harshly
sehr	very

ITALIAN	*FRENCH*
assorbente	mou
attaccare	attaquer
audace	audace, audacieux
audizione	audition
avvicinare	approcher, atteindre
bacchetta	baguette
barcollante	oscillant
basso, grave	bas, profund
battere il tempo	battre la mesure
batteria	batterie
battito	battement
bemolle	bémol
bis	encore
bocca chiusa	bouche fermé
bravura	bravoure, courage
brillante	brillant
brio	verve, élan
brontolare	bourdonner
brusco, bruscamente	brusque, brusquement
buffo	comique
cadenza, chiusa	cadence, terminaison
cadenzale	cadentiel
calmando	calmant
calmato	tranquille, calme

GERMAN	ENGLISH
schallweich	soft [texture]
anspielen, einsatzen	attack (to)
beherzt, kühn	audacious, bold
Vorsingen	audition
erreichen	approach, reach (to)
Taktstock	baton
schwankend	swaying
tief	deep, low
Taktschlagen	beat time (to)
Batterie	percussion section
Schlag, Schwebung	beat
Erniedrigunszeichen	flat [sign]
Zugabe	encore, again
brummstimmen	humming [with closed mouth]
bravour, beherzt	bravura, courage
brillant, glänzend	brilliant
Schmiss	verve
brummen	hum (to)
barsch, heftig	brusquely, abruptly
komisch	comical
Schluss, Endung	cadence, close
kadenzierend	cadencing
beruhingend	calming
gelassen, beruhigend	calm, calmly

ITALIAN	*FRENCH*
cantabile, cantando	chantant
cantante	chanteur
cantare insieme	chanter avec
cantarellare	fredonner
canto funebre	chant funèbre
canto-parlato	sprechgesang
canzone	mélodie
capriccioso	capricieux
caratteristica	caractéristque
carezzando	caressant
carta da musica	papier à musique
cedendo	en cédent
cesura	césure
chiamata	réplique
chiaro, nettamente	net, clair
chiave	clef, clé
chiuso	étouffé
ciclo	cycle
cifra	chiffrage
citare	citer
coda	coda
codetta	crochet de la note
come	comme
cominciare	commencement

GERMAN	ENGLISH
gesanglich, singend	melodiously, singing
Sänger	singer, vocalist
mitsingen	sing with (to)
trällern	trill (to), warble (to)
Grabgesang, Todeslied	dirge, funeral song
Sprechgesang	speech-song, inflected speech
Lied	song
launenhaft	capricious
Merkmal	characteristic, feature
kosend, schmeichelnd	caressing, flattering
Notenpapier	manuscript paper
nachgebend	holding back
Einschnitt	caesura, cut
Stichwort	cue
deutlich, klar	clear, distinct
Schlüssel	clef
gestopft	stopped [horn]
Kreis	cycle, circle
Ziffer	figure
zitieren	quote (to)
Abschluss	coda
Notenfahne	tail, flag, [of a note]
wie	as
Anfang, Eintretend	beginning

ITALIAN	*FRENCH*
comodo	commodément
composizione	composition
con, col, colla	avec
concitato	excité, animé
congiungere	coller
congiunto, di grado	par degrés conjoints
consolante	consolant
contadinesco	villageois
contare	compter
contrappunto	contrepoint
controcanto	contre-thème
controsoggetto	contre-sujet
copione	scénario
corda	corde
coro	choeur
corona, fermata	pause, fermata
cortigianesco	de cour
creare	créer
crescendo	crescendo
croma	croche
da capo, dal segno	depuis le commencement
deciso, decisamente	décidé, avec résolution
declamazione	déclamatoire, narration
decrescendo	en diminuant

GERMAN	ENGLISH
gemächlich,	comfortable, leisurely
Tonsatz	composition
mit	with
agitirt, erregt	excited, stirred
kleben	splice (to)
schrittweise	stepwise
tröstend	consoling
bauernlich	rustic, country-like
zählnen	count (to)
Kontrapunkt	counterpoint
Gegenmelodie	counter-melody
Gegensatz	countersubject
Drehbuch, Szenarium	scenario
Saite	string
Chor	chorus, choir
Fermate	hold, pause
höfisch	courtly
schaffen	create (to)
lauter werdend	louder gradually
Achtelnote	eighth-note
Anfang [von]	repeat from the beginning
bestimmt, entschieden	resolutely, decisively
Deklamation, Rezitativ	declamation, recitative
leiser werdend	softer, gradually

ITALIAN	*FRENCH*
deliberatamente	régulié
descendere, abbassare	descendre, abaisser
devoto	pieusement
di	de
di danza	dansant
di fuoco	fougueux
di tre battute	à trois temps
diapason	diapason standard
diatonico	diatonique
dimenuendo, scemando	diminuendo, en diminuant
diminuire	diminuer
diminuire	diminuer
dirigere	diriger
discendente	descendant
disco	disque
discordia	désaccordé
disinvolto	alerte
disperato	désesperé
dissonanza	dissonant
distendire	détendre
distinto, chiaro	nettement, distinctement
diteggiatura	doigté
divertimento	divertissement
divisi	divisé

GERMAN	ENGLISH
bedächtig	unhurried
absteigen	descend, lower
andächtig	devoutedly
von	of
tänzerisch	dancing
hitzig	hot, fiery, impetuous
dreitaktig	three measure phrases
Normalton	standard pitch
diatonisch	diatonic
abnehmend, leiser werdend	dying away, getting softer
abschwellen	decrease [in loudness]
verkleinern, diminuieren	diminish (to)
dirigieren	conduct (to)
abwärts	downward
Schallplatte	disc, recording
Diskordanz	discordant, out of tune
ungezwungen	easy going
verzweifelt	desperately
Dissonanz	dissonance
entspannen	relax (to)
bestimmt, deutlich	distinct,clear
Fingersatz	fingering
Divertimento	divertisement
geteilt	divided

ITALIAN	FRENCH
dolce, raddolcendo	doucement, doux
dolente, dolore	dolent, triste
dolente	triste
doloroso	douloureaux
doppio	double
doppio colpo di lingua	double articulation
drammatico	dramatique
durata	duré
durezza, asprezza	dureté
editore	éditeur
enarmonico	enharmonique
enfasi	accent
enfatico	emphatique
entrée	empressé, hâter
entusiasmo	enthousiasme
episodio	couplet
equabile	égal
eroico	héroique
esaltare	célébrer
esecuzione	exécution
esequies	obsèques
esercitare	exercise
esile	fin
espirare	expirer

GERMAN	ENGLISH
zart, süss	sweetly, softly
schmerzhaft	sorrowful, pathetic
dolente	doleful
schmerzlich	sad, painful
doppelt	doubled
Doppelzunge	double tonguing
dramatisch	dramatic
Laufzeit	duration, playing time
Härte	harshness
Verleger	publisher
enharmonisch	enharmonic
Schwerpunkt	stress
nachdrücklich	emphatically
Einsatz	cue, entry
Enthusiasmus	enthusiasm
Couplet	episode
gleichmässig	equal
heroisch	heroic
erhaben	extol, praise
Ausführung	performance
Exequien	obsequies
üben	exercise (to)
dünn	thin, reedy
ausatmen	exhale

ITALIAN	FRENCH
espressivo	esspressivo
estensione vocale	registre
estensione	ambitus
estensione	ambitus
estinguendo, mancando	diminuant, éteindre
eufonico	euphonie
falsa	faux
falsetto	fausset
falso bordone	faux-bourdon
fanfara	fanfare, sonnerie
fantasia	fantaisie
feltro	feutre
fermata, corona	point d'orgue
fermo	ferme
feroce	féroce, sauvage
feroce	sauvage, féroce
fervido	ardemment
fervido	fervido
festoso, festivo	joyeux, festivo
fiacca, debole	faible
fiato, respiro	souffle
fiero, fieramente	fier, fièrement
fiero, fieramente	fuer, fiêrement
figurare	orner, figurer

GERMAN	ENGLISH
ausdrucksvoll	expressively
Stimmumfang	range [vocal]
Raum	range
Umfang	range, compass
verlöschend	fading, dying away
Wohlhlang	euphonious
falsch	false
Falsett	falsetto [voice]
Fauxbourdon	fauxbourdon
Tusch	flourish, fanfare
Fantasie	fantasia
Filz	felt
Halt, Fermate	hold, fermata
fest	firmly
wild	ferocious, wild
feroce, wild	wild, ferocious
inbrünstig	fervently
fervido, inbrüstig	fervently
festlich, freudig	merry, festive
schwach	feeble
Atem	breath
stolz	proudly, fiercely
fiero, stolz	proudly, fiercely
figurieren	ornament, embellish (to)

ITALIAN	*FRENCH*
filo	fil
fine	fin
fischiare	siffler
flebile	plaintif, triste
flottuante	flottant
focoso	fougue [avec]
fondere	mélanger
fonte	source
forte	forte, à haut voix
forzare, rinforzare	forcer
frase, periodo	partie, période
frenetico	frénetique
frequenza	fréquence
fresco	fraichement
frivolo	frivole
frontespizio	page de titre
frullato	articulation double
fuga a specchio	fugue en miroir
galop, galoppo	galop
gambo della note	queue de la note
garbato	gracieux
gemendo	plaintif
giocoso	joyeux
gioioso	joyeux, gai

GERMAN	ENGLISH
Garn	thread
Schluss, Ende	end
pfeifen	whistle (to)
klagend	mournful, plaintive
flottant	floating
feurig	fiery
mischen	blend (to)
Quelle	origin, source
forte, laut	loud, strong
forcieren	force, push [the sound]
Satz	period [form]
frenetico, rasend	madly, frenetically
Frequenz	frequency
frisch	freshly
frivol	frivolous
Titelblatt	title page
Flatterzunge	flutter-tonguing
Spiegelfuge	mirror fugue
Galopp	gallop
Notenhals	stem [of a note]
zierlich	polite, graceful
gemendo	lamenting
spasshaft, lustig	merry, jocular
fröhlich, lebhaft	joyous

ITALIAN	*FRENCH*
gioioso	plaisant, joyeux
giubbilose	jubilant
giusto	juste, parfait
giusto	précis, exact
glissando	glissando, en glissant
grado	degré
granire	détacher
grave, pesante	lent, avec gravité
grazioso	aimable, gracieux
gusto [con]	goét avec
imboccatura	embouchure
imitazione	imitation
impazientemente	impatiemment
imperfetto	imparfait
impetuoso	précipité
imponente	imposant
improvvisare	improviser
in battere	frappé
incoerente	incohérent
incompleto	incomplet
indebolendo	affaiblissant
indicato	indicatif
inflessione della voce	inflexion de la voix

GERMAN	ENGLISH
jovialisch	merrily, cheerful
jubelnd	jubilant
rein	perfect [interval]
genau	exact
gleitend	glissando, sliding
Schritt	step
artikulieren	articulate (to)
schwer	solemn, heavy, slow
anmuthig, graziös	gracefully
geschmackvoll	stylishly
Ansatz, Mondloch	embouchure
Nachahmung	imitation
ungeduldig	impatiently
imperfekt	imperfect
heftig, stürmish	impetuous
imponierend	imposing in style
fantasieren	improvise (to)
abtaktig	downbeat
unzusammen-hüngend	incoherent, unconnected
unvollstädig	incomplete
schwächer	weaken
Andeutung	indication
Sprechmelodie	vocal inflection, speech-melody

ITALIAN	FRENCH
inflessione	inflexion
inno	chanson laudative
innocente	innocemment
inquietante	inquiet, agité
insistamente	insistence [avec]
inspirare	respirer
inspirare	respirer
intavolatura	tablature
intavolatura	tablature
intenditore	connaisseur
intensificare	intensifier
interpolare	insérer
interpretare	interpréter
interprtazione	interprétation
intonare	entonner
intonazione	intonation
inudibile	inaudible
ironico	ironiquement
irrequieto	inquiet, agité
irresoluto	indécis
isolante	insonorisé
ispirazione	inspiration, enthousiasme
istruzione	enseignement

GERMAN	ENGLISH
Stimmfall	inflection
Lobegesang	hymn [of praise]
Unschuld	innocently
ruhelos, unheimlich	restless, uneasy
inständig	urgently
einatmen	inhale (to)
Luftholen	inhale (to)
Intabulierung	intabulation
Tabulatur	tablature
Kenner	connoisseur
steigern	intensify (to)
einschieben	interpolate (to)
interpretieren	interpret
Vortrag	interpretation
intonieren	intone (to)
Intonation	intonation
unhörbar	inaudible
ironisch	ironical
unruhig, heftig bewegt	nervous, restless
unentschieden	undecided [in style]
schalldicht	soundproof
begeisterung	inspiration, enthusiasm
Unterricht	instruction, lesson

ITALIAN	*FRENCH*
languendo	langueur
languendo	langueur
languido	languissant
largo ma non troppo	mais pas trop lent
legato	lié
legatura	ligature
leggiero	facile
leggio	pupitre
lestezza	agilité
levare	éloigner
libero	libre
librettista	auteur
lieto	aisé
linea	ligne
linea	ligne
lontano	éloigné
lustro	éclat
macabro	macabre
maestoso	grand
maestoso	majestueux
magnifico	magnifique
malignamente	espièglement
mancando	diminuer, eteindre

GERMAN	ENGLISH
müde, schmachtend, erschlaffen	languishing
müde, schmachtend	languishing
schmachtend	languidly
mässig langsam	slow but not too much
gebunden	slurred, tied
Bindeklappe	slur
leicht	lightly
Notenpult, Notenständer	music stand
beweglichkeit	agility, quickness
wegschaffen	to take off [remove]
frei	free
Textverfasser	author, librettist
froh	glad, joyous
Linie	line [of a staff]
Zeile	line
entfernt	remote
Glanz	brilliance
schauerlich	macabre
grossartig	grand, great
majestätisch	majestic
magnifico, prächtig	magnificent
schalkhaft	roguishly
hinsterbend	dying away

ITALIAN	*FRENCH*
marcato	marqué
marcia	marche
martellato	martelé
marziale	martial
melodia	air, mélodie
melodia	mélodie
melodramma	mélodrame
menestrello	ménestrel
mesto	douloureaux, triste
mezzo	assez
militare	militaire
minacciosamente	minacciosamente
minore	mineur
misterioso	mystérieusement
misura	mesure, tempo
misurato, a battuta	mesure, à la mesure
modello	modèle
moderato	modéré
modulazione	modulation
molto sentimento (con)	beaucoup de sentiment [avec]
mordente	mordant
mordente superiore	pincé
morendo, mancando	diminuer, eteindre
mormorando	murmurant

GERMAN	ENGLISH
markiert	marked, accented
Marsch	march
hämmernd	hammered
kriegerisch	martial
Weise	tune, melody
Melodik	melody
Melodram	melodrama
Spielmann	minstrel
traurig	sad, mournful
ziemlich	fairly
militärisch	military
bedrohlich, drohend	threateningly
Moll	minor [mode]
geheimnisvoll	mysteriously
Takt	beat, bar
abgemessen	strict time, measured
Modell, Vorlage	pattern, model
mässig, gehend	moderately, restrained
Modulation	modulation
gefühlvoll	full of feeling
Mordant	mordant [ornament]
Schneller, Praller	inverted mordent
hinsterbend, ersterbend	dying away
murmelnd, gehaucht	whispering, murmuring

ITALIAN	FRENCH
mosso	mosso
motetto	motet
motivo	motif
moto	mouvement
moto contrario	mouvement contraire
moto obliquo	mouvement oblique
movimento	mouvement
musica	musique
negligente	insouciant
nobile	noblement
non accentato	non accentué
non preparato	non préparé
non tonale	atonal
nona	neuvième
nonetto	nonet
nota tenuta	note tenue
notazione quadrata	notation carrée
notazione sillabica	notation syllabique
notturno	nocturne
numero di battute	numéro de la mesure
obbligato	obligé
ondeggiando	ondoyant
onorario	cachet
orecchio	oreille

GERMAN	ENGLISH
bewegt	moving, animated
Motette	motet
Motiv	motive
Bewegung	motion, movement
Gegenbewegung	contrary motion
Seitenbewegung	oblique motion
Satz	movement [of a work]
Tonkunst	music, tonal art
gleichgültigkeit	carelessly, with indifference
edel	noble, grand
unbetonnt	unaccented
unvorbereitet	unprepared
nichttonal	non-tonal
None	ninth
Nonett	nonet
Pfundnote	long note
Quadratnotation	square notation
Tonsilbenschrift	syllabic notation
Abendlied, Nocturne	nocturne
Taktzahl	bar number
obligat	obligatory
wogend	undulating, wavering
Gage	fee
Ohr	ear

ITALIAN	*FRENCH*
ossia	ou
ottetto	octuor
pacato	placide
parafrasi	paraphrase
parlando, parlante	parler
parte, voce	voix, partie
particella	partie
partitura, spartito	partition
passaggio	passage
pastorale	pastorale
patètico	pathétique
pauroso	craintif, timide
pausa	silence, pause
pentagramma	portée
pentrante, acuto	pénétrant
periodo	période
piacevole, gradito	plaisant, charmant
piano	doux
piatto portadischi	plateau
pieno	plein, pleine
pieta, pietoso	dolent
più	plus
pizzicare, strappare	pincer
pizzicato	pincé

GERMAN	ENGLISH
oder	or
Oktett	octet
ruhig, sanft	calm, placid
Umspielung	paraphrase
redend, sprechen	speaking
Stimme	voice, part
Particell	short score
Partitur, Sparte	score
Durchgang	transition
Pastorale, Hirtenlied	pastoral
pathetisch	pathetic
angstvoll	timidly
Pause	rest
Liniensystem	staff, stave
durchdringend	penetrating, shrill
Periode	period
angenehm, gefüllig	pleasing
leise	soft [dynamics]
Plattenteller	turntable
volltsnig, rund	full [as in full voice]
Mitleid	pity, mercy
mehr	more
zupfen, anreissen	pluck (to)
gezupft	plucked

ITALIAN	FRENCH
placido	placide
poco a poco	peu a peu, graduellement
podio	podium
poeta	parolier, poète
poggiato	appuyer
polacca	polanaise
politematico	polythématique
pomposo	pompeux
ponticello	chevalet
posizione	position
possènte, potente	puissant, fort
postludio	postlude
preludio	ouverture
preparazione	préparation
prestito	emprunt
presto	vite, rapide
primo violino	premier violon
profano	profane
prolungamento	prolongement
proposta	antécédent
prova	répétition
provare	entrainer
punta	pointe
punto, puntato	point, pointé

GERMAN	ENGLISH
friedlich	placid
allmählich, gradweisse	little by little, gradually
Podium	podium, rostrum
Textdichter	poet, lyricist
aufhalten	leaned upon
Polonaise	polonaise
vielthemig	polythematic
pompös	pompous
Steg	bridge
Lage	spacing [of a chord]
mächtig	mighty, powerful
Nachspiel	epilogue
Vorspiel	overture, prelude
Vorbereitung	preparation
Entlehnung	borrowing
schnell	fast
Primgeige	first violin
weltlich	secular
Tastenfessel	sustaining pedal
Proposta, Leitmelodie	antecedent [canon]
Probe	rehearsal
korrepetieren	coach (to)
Spitze	tip, point
Punkt, punktiert	dot, dotted

ITALIAN	FRENCH
quarta	quarte
quartetto	quatuor
quartina	quartolet
quinta	quinte
quinte giuste	quintes justes
quintetto	quintette
quintina	quintolet
raccolta	collection
rallentare	ralentir
rapidissimo	rapidement
rappresentare	représenter
ravvivando	pressant
recensire	recenser
recitare	réciter
recitativo	récitatif
regia	régie
regista	régisseur
registrare	enregistrer
registrazione	enregistrement
regolare	régler
reinterpretazione	équivoque
requiem	Requiem, messe funèbre
respiro	respiration
restare indietro	retarder

GERMAN	ENGLISH
Quart	fourth [interval]
Quartett	quartet
Quartole	quadruplet
Quint	fifth [interval]
quintenrein	perfect fifths [in]
Quintett	quintet
Quintole	quintuplet
Sammlung	collection
nachlassen	slow down (to)
rasch	rapidly
aufführen	perform (to)
beschleunigung	quicken
rezensieren	review, criticize (to)
rezitieren	recite (to)
Rezitativ	recitative
Regie	production, stage direction
Spielleiter	producer, artistic director
einspielen	record (to)
Aufnahme	recording
regulieren	regulate
Umdeutung	reintepretation
Totenmesse	Mass for the dead
Luftpause	breathing pause
nachhinken	lag behind (to)

ITALIAN	FRENCH
retrogrado	rétrograde
ricercare	ricercar
ricorrere	revenir
ridotto	réduire
riduzione	abbréviation
rielaborare	retoucher
rigido, teso	rigide, tendu
rinforzando	renforcent
rinforzato	renforcé
risoluto	décidé, décisif
risolvere	résoudre
risonante	résonnant
risonanza	résonance
risposta	réponse
risposta	réponse
ristampa	reproduction
ritardando, rallentando, raffrenando	ralentissant, étendre,
ritardare	hésiter
ritardo	retard
ritenuto	retenu
ritmo	rythme
ritornello	refrain
rivedare	réviser

GERMAN	ENGLISH
krebsgängig	retrograde, crabwise
Ricercar	ricercare
wiederkehren	recur (to). return (to)
reduzieren	reduced, arranged
verkürzung	abbreviate (to), shorten (to)
überarbeiten	rework (to), revise (to)
straff	tense, rigid, taut
stärker werdend	strengthening
verstärkt	reinforced, strenghthened
gewiss	bold, determined
auflösen	resolve (to)
resonanzföhig	resonant
Nachklingen	echo, resonance
Antwort	answer, consequence
Risposta	consequent
Nachdruck	reprint
zurückhatten, langsamer werdend	slowing down
zögern	hesitate (to), retard (to)
Vorhalt	suspension
ritenuto	held back
Rhythmus	rhythm
Wiederholung	chorus, refrain
revidieren	revise (to)

ITALIAN	FRENCH
riverberante	dur
riverberazione	réverbération
rivolto	inversion
rubato	rubato
rumore	bruit
salendo	ascendant
salmo	psaume
saltellare	sauter
scala	gamme, échelle
scandire	scander
scherzando	badinant
scintillante	brillant
scordato	désaccordé
scorrendo, scorrevole	coulant, facile
scorrevolezza	vèlocitè
scucito	détaché
scuotere, agitere	secouer, agiter
scurito	couvert, voilé
secco	sec, séche
segnatura	signature
segni di ripetizione	signe de reprise
segno	signe
segno d'indicazione	signe de la mesure

GERMAN	ENGLISH
schallhart	hard
Nachhall	reverberation
Umkehrung	inversion
rubato	robbed rhythm
Geräusch	noise
aufwärtsgehend	ascending, upwards
Psalm	psalm
höpsen	hop, leap (to)
Tonleiter	scale
skandieren	scan
scherzhaft	joking
funkelnd	sparkling
verstimmt	out of tune
fliessend	flowing, fluid
Geläufigkeit	velocity
abgezetzt	unconnected, non legato
schütteln	shake (to)
gedeckt	muffled [voice]
trocken, kurz	dry
Signatur	signature
Wiederholungszeichen	repeat sign
Zeichen	mark, sign
Taktvorzeichen	time signature

ITALIAN	*FRENCH*
segue	suivre, enchaînez
seguito	séquence
semibrevis	semi-brève
semicroma	double croche
semitono	demi-ton
semplice	simplement
sentito	intime
senza	sans
sequenza	séquence
serenata	sérénade
serioso	sérieux
sesta	sixte
sestetto	sextuor
sestina	sextolet
settimino	septuor
severo, rigoroso	sévère
sezione, parte	section, partie
sforzando, sforzato	renforçant
sibilante	lettre sifflante
sillaba	syllabe
sillabico	syllabique
simile	similaire
simpatico	sympathetique
sincope	syncope

GERMAN	ENGLISH
folgen	continue [without break]
Folge	progression
Semibrevis, Ganze	whole note
Sechzehntelnote	sixteenth-note
Halbton	semitone, half tone
einfach	simply
innig	heartfelt
ohne	without
Sequenz	sequence
Ständchen	serenade
ernst	serious
Sexte	sixth
Sextett	sextet
Sextole	sextuplet
Septett	septet
streng	strict
Teil	section, part
starken akzentuiertem	forced, accented
Zischlaut	sibilant
Silbe	syllable
syllabisch	syllabic
ebenfalls	similar, in a like manner
mitklingend	sympathetic
Synkopierung	syncopation

ITALIAN	*FRENCH*
sinfonia	symphonie
singhiozzando	pleurant
slancio	impulsion, vitesse
smanicare	démancher
smorzarsi	s'évanouir
snèllo	légér, agilement
soave	doucement
soffiato	murmuré
soggetto	sujet
solenne	solennel
solfeggio	solfége
sollecitando	empressé, hâter
solo	seul
sommesso	voilé
sonata	sonate
sonata da camera	sonata de chambre
sonata da chiesa	sonate d'église
sordino	sourdine
sordo	sourd
sospiro	soupir
sostenare	soutenir
sostenuto, tenendo	tenu, soutenu
sostituto	doublure
specie	espèce

GERMAN	ENGLISH
Symphonie	symphony
schluchzend	sobbing
impuls, Stosskraft,	impetus, outburst
demanchieren	shift [position]
abklingen	fade out, die away
hurtig, leicht	nimble, agile
sanft	gently, suavely
hauchig	breathy
Thema	subject, theme
feierlich	solemnly
Solfeggio	solfeggio
eilen, hastig, triebend	hastening, pressing
allein	alone
demütig	weak [voice]
Sonate	sonata
Kammersonate	chamber sonata
Kirchensonata	church sonata
Dämpfer	mute
kurzatmig	dull [in tone]
Seufzer	sigh
stützen	support (to)
gehalten, getragen	sustained
Ersatzspieler	understudy
Gattung	species

ITALIAN	FRENCH
sperdendosi [perdendosi]	en mourant
spiccato	sautillé
spirituale	spirituel
staccato	détaché
stampa	impression
stanghetta	barre
stato d'animo	climat
stile, scrittura	style, écriture
stonare	détonner
strappare	pincer
strepitoso	bruyant
stretto	strette
stridento, strillo	strident
strimpellare	tapoter
strimpello	tapotage
stringendo	pressant
strofa	strophe
strumentare	instrumenter
struttura	structure
subito	subitement
successivamente	successivement
suggeritore	souffleur
suonare con l'arco	jouer avec l'archet

GERMAN	ENGLISH
verhallend	dying away
Springbogen	bouncing [bow]
geistlich	spiritual, sacred
abgestossen	detached
Druck	print, edition
Taktstrich	barline
Stimmung	mood
Satzart	setting, style
detonieren	waver in pitch (to), sing off pitch (to)
anreissen	pluck (to)
lärmend	noisy
Engführung	stretto
schreiend	sharp, shrill
klimpern	strum (to)
Geklimper	strumming
drängend	quickening, urging on
Strophe	stanza
instrumentieren	orchestrate (to)
Struktur	structure
plötzlich, sofort	suddenly
hintereinander	successively
Souffleur	prompter
streichen	bow (to)

ITALIAN	FRENCH
suonare	jouer
suonare	sonner
suono	son
sussurando	murmurant
svelto	vif, agilement
sviluppo, svolgimento	développement
tablatura	tablature
taglio linea supplementare	ligne supplémentaire
taglio	coupure
taglio	saut
tardo, tardamento	lent
tastiera	clavier
tasto	touche
tematico	thématique
tempestoso	orageux
tempo	temps
tenore	ténor
tensione	tension
tenuto	tenue
teorico, teoretico	théorique
terza	tierce
terzetto	trio
terzina	triolet
testo	récitant

GERMAN	ENGLISH
spielen	play (to)
erklingen	sound (to)
Klang, Schall	tone, sound
säuselnd	whispering
behende	agile, nimbly
Dürchführung	development [thematic]
Griffnotation	tablature
Hilfslinie	ledger line
Streichung	cut
Sprung	leap, skip
langsam	slow
Klaviatur	keyboard
Taste	note, key
thematisch	thematic
stürmisch	tempestuous
Zeitmass	meter
Tenor	tenor
Spannung	tension
Bindung	tie
theoretisch	theoretical
Terz	third
Terzett	trio
Triole	triplet
Testo	narrator

ITALIAN	*FRENCH*
tetro, cupo	sombre, triste
timbro	timbre
tintinnare	tinter
tocco	attaque
tonale	tonal
tonalità	tonalité
tonica	tonique
tono	tonalité
tono (intero)	ton entier
tosto	bientôt, vite
trascinando, stentando	traînant
trascripzione	transcription
trascrivere	arranger
trasognato	comme dans un songe
traspotare	transposer
tratto d'unione	barre transversale
tremendo	terrible
tremolando	tremblant
tremolare	chevroter
tremolo	trémolo
triade	triade
trillo	trille
triste	triste
troncare	arrêter

GERMAN	ENGLISH
düster	gloomy, dismal
Tonfarbe	tone color
bimmeln	tinkle (to)
Spielart	touch
tonlich	tonal
Tonalität	tonality
Tonika	tonic
Tonart	key, mode, tonality
Ganzton	whole tone
bald, schnell	soon, quick
schleppend	dragging
übertragung	transcription
bearbeiten	arrange (to)
traümerisch	dreamily
transponieren	transpose (to)
Notenbalken	beam, cross-bar
enorm, riesig	tremendous
zitternd	trembling
wackeln	wobble (to)
Tremolo	tremolo
Dreiklang	triad
Triller	trill, shake
wehmütig	sad, mournful
abbrechen	break off

ITALIAN	FRENCH
troppo	trop
tutti	tous
udibile	perceptible
udire, ascoltare	entendre, écouter
ultimo	dernier
umore	plaisant
undicesima	onziàme
unisono	unisson
vago	vague
valore della note	valeur de la note
velato	voilé, brumeux
vellutato	velouté
versione	version
vibrare	vibrer
vibrato	vibrato
virtuosità	virtuosité
virtuoso	virtuose
vivo	vivement
vocalizzo	vocalise
volante	volant
volti!	tournez [la page!]
zelo	zèle
zingaro	tsigane

GERMAN	ENGLISH
zu sehr	too much
alle	all
hörbar	audible
hören	hear (to)
endlich	last, ultimate
launig	humor
Undezime	eleventh
Einklang, Prim	unison
unbestimmt	vague
Notenwert	note value
verschliert	veiled, husky [voice]
samtig	velvety
Fassung	version
schwingen, vibrieren	vibrate (to)
Bebung	vibrato
Kunstfertigkeit	virtuosity
virtuos	masterly, virtuoso
lebendig, lebhaft	lively
Vocalise	vocalise
fliegend	rushing
umblättern!	turn [the page!]
zele, eifger	zeal
Zigeuner	gypsy

FRENCH

FRENCH	GERMAN
à	bis
à deux	zwei Gesang
à la mesure	abgemess
à peine	kaum
à volanté	ad libitum, belieben
abaisser	absteigen
abbréviation	Verkürzung
accelerant, en	eiland
accéléré	beschleunigt
accent	Schwerpunkt
accentué, appuyé	betont
acceso, avec fougue	feurig
acciaccatura	Quetschung
accolade	Klammer
accompagner	begleiten
accord	Akkord
accordé	abgestimmt
accorder	einstimmen
acoustique	Akustik
adagietto	adagietto
affable	lieberswürdig
affaiblissant	schwächer
affecté	geziert
affligé	betrübt

ITALIAN	ENGLISH
al	to
a due	two voices or instruments
misurato, a battuta	strict time, measured
appena	scarcely, hardly
a libito, beneplacito	freely
abbassarsi	lower (to), descend (to)
riduzione	abbreviation
affrettando	hurrying
accelerato	faster, accelerated
enfasi	stress
accentato	accented, stressed
acceso, focoso	fiery
acciaccatura	acciaccatura [ornament]
graffa	brace, bracket
accompagnare	accompany (to)
accordo	chord
accordato	tuned, pitched
accordare	tune (to)
acustica	acoustics, science of sound
adagietto	adagietto, faster than adagio
affabile	affable, pleasant
indebolendo	weaken
affettato	mannered, affected
afflitto	down-hearted

FRENCH	*GERMAN*
agilité	beweglichkeit
agité	bewegt
aigrement, âpre	rauh, hart-klingend
aimable	graziös
air	Weise, Melodik
alerte	ungezwungen
alla breve	Allabrevetakt
allègre	munter
ambigu	mehrdeutig
ambitus	Umfang, Raum
anacrouse	Auftakt
anche	Rohrblatt
andante, allant	andante, gehend
angoissé	ängstlich
animé	belebt
antécédent	Proposta
antienne	Antiphon
appogiature	Vorschlag
approcher, atteindre	erreichen
ardemment	inbrünstig
arpégé	arpeggiert, gebrochen
arranger	bearbeiten
arrêt, silence	Stillstand
arrêter	abbrechen

ITALIAN	ENGLISH
lestezza	agility, quickness
agitato	agitated
aspramente	harshly
grazioso	gracefully
melodia	tune, melody
disinvolto	easy going
tempo alla breve	cut time
allegro	cheerful, lively
ambiguo	ambiguous
estensione	range, compass
anacrusi	upbeat
ancia	reed
andante	walking
affannato	anguished, distressed
animato	brisk, animated
antecedent	antecedent [canon]
antifona	antiphon
appogiatura	appogiatura [ornament]
avvicinare	approach (to), reach (to)
fervido	fervently
arpeggiando, arpeggiato	broken, arpeggiated
trascrivere	arrange (to)
arresto	stop
troncare	break off (to)

FRENCH	*GERMAN*
articulation double	Flatterzunge
articuler	absetzen
artificel	künstlich
artistique	künstlerich
ascendant	aufwärtsgehend, ansteigend
assez	ziemlich
atonal	nichttonal
attaque, frappe	Spielart, Anschlag
attaquer	anspielen, einsatzen
audacieux, hardi	kühn, keck
audible	hörbar
audition	Vorsingen
augmenté	übermässig
augmenter	anschwellen
auteur	Textverfasser
avec	mit
badinant	scherzhaft
baguette	Taktstock
baisser	erniedrigen
barre transversale	Notenbalken
barre de mesure	Taktstrich
bas, profund	tief
battement	Schlag, Schwebung
batterie	Batterie

ITALIAN	*ENGLISH*
frullato	flutter-tonguing
articolare	separate (to), articulate (to)
artificale	artificel
artistico	artistic
salendo	ascending, rising
mezzo	fairly
non tonale	atonal
tocco	touch, action
attaccare	attack (to)
ardito, arditamente	bold, courageous
udibile	audible
audizione	audition
aumentato	augmented [interval]
addensare, ispessire	grow louder (to)
librettista	author, librettist
con, col, colla	with
scherzando	joking
bacchetta	baton
abbassare	lower (to), flatten (to)
tratto d'unione	beam, cross-bar
stanghetta	barline
basso, grave	deep, low
battito	beat
batteria	percussion section

FRENCH	*GERMAN*
battre la mesure	Taktschlagen
beaucoup, très	sehr
beaucoup de sentiment (avec)	gefühlvoll
bécarre	Auflösungszeichen
bémol	Erniedrigungszeichen
bien	gut
bientôt, vite	bald, schnell
bourdonner	brummen
bravoure, courage	bravour, beherzt
brillant	glänzend
broderies	Singmanieren
bruit	Geräusch
brusque, brusquement	barsch, heftig
bruyant	lärmend
cachet	Gage
cadence, terminaison	Schluss, Endung
cadentiel	kadenzierend
calmant	beruhingend
capricieux	launenhaft
caractéristque	Merkmal
caressant	schmeichelnd
carillonner	läuten
césure	Einschnitt

ITALIAN	ENGLISH
battere il tempo	beating time
assai	very
molto sentimento (con)	full of feeling
bequadro [doppio]	natural [sign]
bemolle	flat [sign]
bene	well
tosto	soon, quick
brontolare	hum (to)
bravura	bravura, courage
brillante	brilliant
abbellimenti vocali	vocal ornaments
rumore	noise
brusco, bruscamente	brusquely, abruptly
strepitoso	noisy
onorario	fee
cadenza, chiusa	cadence, close
cadenzale	cadencing
calmando	calming
capriccioso	capricious
caratteristica	characteristic, feature
scarezevole, lusingando	caressingly
scampanare	chime (to), peal (to)
cesura	caesura, cut

FRENCH	*GERMAN*
changeant (en)	abwechselnd
chanson laudative	Lobegesang
chant funèbre	Grabgesang, Todeslied
chantant	gesanglich, singend
chanter	singen
chanteur, chanteuse	Sänger, Sängerin
charmant	angenehm,
chef d'oeuvre	Kunstwerk
chevalet	Steg
chevroter	wackeln
chiffrage	Ziffer
choeur	Chor
chromatique	chromatisch
chuchotant	flüsternd,
citer	zitieren
clavier	Klaviatur
clef, clé	Schlüssel
climat	Stimmuing
coda	Abschluss
colèrique	zornig, erregt
collection	Sammlung
coller	kleben
comique	komisch
comme	wie

ITALIAN	*ENGLISH*
alternando	alternating
inno	hymn [of praise]
canto funebre	dirge, funeral song
cantabile, cantando	melodiously, singing
cantare	sing (to)
cantante	singer, vocalist
piacevole	pleasingly
capolavoro	masterpiece
ponticello	bridge
tremolare	wobble (to)
cifra	figure
coro	chorus, choir
cromatico	chromatic
bisbigliando	whispering
citare	quote (to)
tastiera	keyboard
chiave	clef
stato d'animo	mood
coda	coda
adirato	angered, irate
raccolta	collection
congiungere	splice (to)
buffo	comical
come	as

FRENCH	GERMAN
comme dans un songe	traümerisch
commencement	Anfang, Eintretend
commodément	gemächlich
composition	Tonsatz
compter	zählen
connaisseur	Kenner
consolant	tröstend
consonnant	konsonant
contre-sujet	Gegensatz
contre-thème	Gegenmelodie
contrepoint	Kontrapunkt
copier	anschreiben
corde	Saite
coulant, fluide	fliessend, flüssig
coup	schlag
couplet	Couplet
coupure	Streichung
couvert, voilé	gedeckt, belegt
craintif, timide	angstvoll
créer	schaffen
crescendo	lauter werdend
croche	Achtelnote
crochet de la note	Notenfahne
cycle	Kreis

ITALIAN	ENGLISH
trasognato	dreamily
cominciare	beginning
comodo	comfortable, leisurely
composizione	composition
contare	count (to)
intenditore	connoisseur
consolante	consoling
consonante	consonant
controsoggetto	countersubject
controcanto	counter-melody
contrappunto	counterpoint
copiare	copy (to)
corda	string
scorrendo, scorrevole	flowing, fluent
colpo	beat [an instrument]
episodio	episode
taglio	cut
scurito	muffled [voice]
pauroso	timidly
creare	create (to)
crescendo	louder gradually
croma	eighth-note
codetta	tail, flag [of a note]
ciclo	cycle, circle

FRENCH	*GERMAN*
dansant	tänzerisch
de	von
de cour	höfisch
décidé, décisif	gewiss
déclamation, narration	Deklamation, Rezitativ
dégagé	ungebunden
degré	Schritt
délicat	zart
démancher	demanchieren
demi-cadence	Halbkadenz
demi-ton	Halbton
depuis le commencement	Anfang [von]
dernier	endlich
désaccordé	verstimmt
descendant, en	abwärts
désesperé	verzweifelt
détaché	abgestossen
détendre	entspannen
détonner	detonieren
développement	Fortspinnung
développement thématique	Dürchführung
dextérité	Fertigkeit
diapason standard	Normalton

ITALIAN	ENGLISH
di danza	dancing
di	of
cortigianesco	courtly
risoluto	determined
declamazione	declamation, recitative
sciolto	relaxed, free
grado	step
delicato	delicately
smanicare	shift [position]
semi-cadenza	half-cadence
semitono	semitone, half tone
da capo, dal segno	repeat from the beginning
ultimo	last, ultimate
scordato	out of tune
discendente	downward, descending
disperato	desperately
staccato	detached
distendire	relax (to)
stonare	waver in pitch (to), sing off pitch (to)
sviluppo	continuation
elaborazione tematico	development [thematic]
abilità	dexterity
diapason	standard pitch

FRENCH	*GERMAN*
diatonique	diatonisch
dièse	Erhöhungszeichen
diminuant, éteindre	verlöschend
diminuendo, en diminuant	abnehmend, leiser werdend
diminuer	abschwellen
diminuer	verkleinern, diminuieren
diriger	dirigieren
disque	Schallplatte
dissonance	Dissonanz
divertissement	Divertimento
divisé	geteilt
doigté	Fingersatz
dolente, triste	schmerzhaft
double	doppelt
double articulation	Doppelzunge
double croche	Sechzehntelnote
doublure	Ersatzspieler
doucement, doux	süss, sanft
douloureaux	traend
doux	leise
dramatique	dramatisch
droits d'auteur	Urheberrecht
dur	schallhart
durée	Laufzeit

ITALIAN	ENGLISH
diatonico	diatonic
diesis	sharp [sign]
estinguendo, mancando	fading away
dimenuendo, scemando	dying away, getting softer
diminuire	decrease (to) [dynamics]
diminuire	diminish (to) [interval]
dirigere	conduct (to)
disco	disc, recording
dissonanza	dissonance
divertimento	divertisement
divisi	divided
diteggiatura	fingering
doloroso	doleful
doppio	doubled
doppio colpo di lingua	double tonguing
semicroma	sixteenth-note
sostituto	understudy
dolce, dolcemento	sweetly, gently
addolorato	sorrowful
piano	soft [dynamics]
drammatico	dramatic
diritto d'autore	copyright
riverberante	hard
durata	duration, playing time

FRENCH	*GERMAN*
dureté	Härte
éclat	Glanz
écouter	zuhören
éditeur	Verleger
égal	gleichmässig
en mourant	verhallend
élargissant	breiter werdend
élargissement	Erweiterung
éloigné	entfernt
embouchure	Ansatz, Mondloch
emphatique	nachdrücklich
emprunt	Entlehnung
en berçant	weigend
en cédent	nachgebend
en diminuant	leiser werdend
en mesure	im Tact, im Zeitmas
en mourant	verhallend
encore	Zugabe
encore	wieder, noch
enharmonique	enharmonisch
enregistrement	Aufnahme
enregistrer	einspielen
enseignement	Unterricht
ensemble	zusammen

ITALIAN	ENGLISH
durezza, asprezza	harshness
lustro	lustrous
ascoltare	listen (to)
editore	publisher
equabile, uniforme	even, equal
sperdendosi [perdendosi]	dying away
allargando	broadening
allargamento	expansion, extension
lontano	remote
imboccatura	embouchure
enfatico	emphatically
prestito	borrowing
cullando	rocking
cedendo	holding back
decrescendo	softer, gradually
a tempo	in tempo
sperendosi [perendosi]	dying away
bis	encore
ancora	again
enarmonico	enharmonic
registrazione	recording
registrare	record (to)
istruzione	instruction, lesson
insieme	together

FRENCH	GERMAN
entendre, écouter	hören
entonner	intonieren
entrainer	korrepetieren
équivoque	Umdeutung
espèce	Gattung
espièglement	schalkhaft
esquisse	Entwurf
éteindre	hinsterbend, ersterbend
étouffé	gestopft
étude	Etüde
euphonie	wohlklingend
excessif	übertrieben
excité, animé	agitirt, erregt
exécution	Ausführung
exercer	üben
expirer	ausatmen
expressivo	ausdrucksvoll
faible	schwach
fanfare, sonnerie	Tusch, Fanfare
fantaisie	Fantasie
fausset	Falsett
faux	falsch
faux-bourdon	Fauxbourdon
ferme	fest

ITALIAN	ENGLISH
udire, ascoltare	hear (to)
intonare	intone (to)
provare	coach (to)
reinterpretazione	reintepretation
specie	species
malignamente	roguishly
abbozzo	draft, sketch
morendo, mancando	dying away
chiuso	stopped [horn]
studio	study
eufonico	euphonious
eccessivo	exceedingly
concitato	excited, stirred
esecuzione	performance
esercitare	exercise (to)
espirare	exhale
espressivo	expressively
debole	feeble, weak
fanfara	fanfare, flourish
fantasia	fantasia
falsetto	falsetto [voice]
falsa	false
falso bordone	fauxbourdon
fermo	firmly

FRENCH	*GERMAN*
féroce, sauvage	wild
festivo	festlich, freudig
feutre	Filz
fier, fièrement	stolz
fil	Garn
fin	Ende
fluté	flötemartig
forcer	forcieren
forte, à haut voix	forte, laut
fraichement	frisch
frappé	abtaktig
fredonner	trällern
frénetique	frenetico, rasend
fréquence	Frequenz
frivole	frivol
fugue en miroir	Spiegelfuge
furieux	wütend
gai	lustig
galop	Galopp
gamme, échelle	Tonleiter
gamme pentatonique	Fünftonleiter
glissando, en glissant	gleitend
goét (avec)	geschmackvoll
gracieux	anmutig

ITALIAN	*ENGLISH*
feroce	ferocious, wild
festoso, festivo	festive, merry
feltro	felt
fiero, fieramente	proudly, fiercely
filo	thread
fine	end
flautato	fluty
forzare, rinforzare	force (to), push (to) [the sound]
forte	loud, strong
fresco	freshly
in battere	downbeat
cantarellare	trill (to), warble (to)
frenetico	madly, frenetically
frequenza	frequency
frivolo	frivolous
fuga a specchio	mirror fugue
furioso	furiously
lieto	joyous
galop, galoppo	gallop
scala	scale
scala pentatonica	pentatonic scale
glissando	glissando, sliding
gusto [con]	stylishly
leggiadro	gracefully

FRENCH	GERMAN
grand, majestueux	grossartig, majestätisch
grave	schwer
raveur musicale	Notenstecher
guttural	kehlig
harmonique	Oberton
hausser	erhöhen
haut, aigu	hoch
hauteur	Höhe
hauteur du son	Tonhöhe
héroique	heroisch
hésitant	verzögert
hymnique	hymnisch
imitation	Nachahmung
imparfait	imperfekt
impatiemment	ungeduldig
impétueux	heftig, stürmisch
imposant	imponierend
impression	Druck
improviser	fantasieren
inaudible	unhörbar
incomplet	unvollständig
indécis	unentschieden
indicatif	Andeutung
inflexion	Stimmfall

ITALIAN	ENGLISH
maestoso	grand, majestically
grave, pesante	solemn, slow
incisore di musica	music engraver
gutturale	guttural, throaty
armonico	overtone
alzare	raise (to), sharpen
alto, acuto	high
altezza	upper notes, treble
altezza del suono	pitch, pitch level
eroico	heroic
allentato	delayed
innodico	hymn-like
imitazione	imitation
imperfetto	imperfect
impazientemente	impatiently
impetuoso	impetuous
imponente	imposing in style
stampa	print, edition
improvvisare	improvise (to)
inudibile	inaudible
incompleto	incomplete
irresoluto	undecided [in style]
indicato	indication
inflessione	inflection

FRENCH	*GERMAN*
inflexion de la voix	Sprechmelodie, Tonfall
inquiet, agité	unruhig
insérer	einschieben
insistance [avec]	inständig
insonorisé	schalldicht
inspiration	Einfall
instrumenter	instrumentier-en, besetzen
intensifier	steigern
interprétation	Vortrag, Auffassung
intervalle	Interval
intime	innig
intonation	Intonation
inversion	Umkehrung
jouer	spielen
jouer avec l'archet	streichen
joyeux	spasshaft
jubilant	jubelnd
juste, parfait	rein, genau
lâcher	loslassen
languissant	schmachtend
largo	breit
légér, facile	leicht, hurtig
lent	langsam

ITALIAN	ENGLISH
inflessione della voce	vocal inflection, speech-melody
irrequieto	nervously
interpolare	interpolate (to)
insistemente	urgently
isolante	soundproof
ispirazione	inspiration
strumentare	orchestrate (to), score (to)
intensificare	intensify (to)
interpretazione	interpretation
intervallo	interval
sentito	heartfelt
intonazione	intonation
rivolto	inversion
suonare	play (to)
suonare con l'arco	bow (to)
giocoso	joyful
giubbilose	jubilant
giusto	perfect, exact
abbandonare	release (to)
languido	languidly
largo	broad[ly]
leggiero, agevole	lightly, easily
adagio	slow

FRENCH	*GERMAN*
lettre sifflante	Zischlaut
libre	frei
lié	gebunden
ligne	Linie
ligne supplémentaire	Hilfslinie
lourd	wuchtig
lutrin	Chorpult
macabre	schauerlich
magnifique	magnifico, prächtig
majeur	gross
manuscrit	Handschrift
marche	Marsch
marqué	markiert
martelé	hämmernd
martial	kriegerisch
mélanger	mischen
mélodie, chanson	Lied, Melodie
mélodrame	Melodram
ménestrel	Spielmann
mesure, tempo	Takt
militaire	militärisch
minacciosamente	bedrohlich, drohend
mineur	klein
mineur	Moll

ITALIAN	*ENGLISH*
sibilante	sibilant
libero	free
legato	slurred, tied
linea	line [of a staff]
taglio linea supplementare	ledger line
pesante	heavy
leggio	lectern
macabro	macabre
magnifico	magnificent
maggiore	major [interval]
manuscritto	manuscript
marcia	march
marcato	marked, accented
martellato	hammered
marziale	martial
fondere	blend (to)
canzone, melodia	song, melody
melodramma	melodrama
menestrello	minstrel
misura	bar, measure
militare	military
minacciosamente	threateningly
minore	minor [interval]
minore	minor [mode]

FRENCH	*GERMAN*
modèle	Modell, Vorlage
modéré	mässig, gehend
modulation	Modulation
moins	weniger
mordant	Mordent
mormorato, murmuré	hauchig
mosso	bewegt
motet	Motette
motif	Motiv
mou	schallweich
mouvement contraire	Gegenbewegung
mouvement oblique	Seitenbewegung
mouvement	Bewegung
mouvement	Satz
murmurant	murmelnd, gehaucht
musique	Tonkunst
musique de chambre	Kammermusik
mystérieusement	geheimnisvoll
net, clair	deutlich, klar
neuvième	None
noble	edel
nocturne	Abendlied, Nocturne
noire	Viertelnote
non accentué	unbetont

ITALIAN	ENGLISH
modello	pattern, model
moderato	moderately, restrained
modulazione	modulation
meno	less
mordente	mordant [ornament]
soffiato	breathy
mosso	moving, animated
motetto	motet
motivo	motive
assorbente	soft [texture]
moto contrario	contrary motion
moto obliquo	oblique motion
moto	motion, movement
movimento	movement [of a work]
mormorando	whispering, murmuring
musica	music, tonal art
musica da camera	chamber music
misterioso	mysteriously
chiaro, nettamente	clear, distinct
nona	ninth [interval]
nobile	noble, grand
notturno	nocturne
semiminima, quarto	quarter note, crotchet
non accentato	unaccented

FRENCH	*GERMAN*
non préparé	unvorbereitet
nonet	Nonett
normal, naturel	natürlich
notation carée	Quadratnotation
notation syllabique	Tonsilbenschrift
note tenue	Pfundnote
numéro de la mesure	Taktzahl
obligé	obligat
obsèques	Exequien
octuor	Oktett
ondoyant	wogend
onzième	Undezime
orageux	stürmisch
oreille	Ohr
ornements	Manieren
orner, figurer	figurieren
ou	oder
ouverture	Vorspiel
page de titre	Titelblatt
papier à musique	Notenpapier
par degrés conjoints	schrittweise
paraphrase	Umspielung
parolier, poète	Textdichter
partie	Particell

ITALIAN	ENGLISH
non preparato	unprepared
nonetto	nonet
naturale, normale	normal, usual
notazione quadrata	square notation
notazione sillabica	syllabic notation
nota tenuta	sustained note
numero di battute	bar number
obbligato	obligatory
esequies	funeral music
ottetto	octet
ondeggiando	undulating, wavering
undicesima	eleventh
tempestoso	tempestuous
orecchio	ear
abbellimenti	ornaments
figurare	ornament (to), embellish (to)
ossia	or
preludio	overture, prelude
frontespizio	title page
carta da musica	manuscript paper
congiunto, di grado	stepwise
parafrasi	paraphrase
poeta	poet, lyricist
particella	short score

FRENCH	GERMAN
partition	Partitur, Sparte
passage	Durchgang
passionné	leidenschaftlich
pastorale	Pastorale, Hirtenlied
pathétique	pathetisch
pénétrant	durchdringend
période, partie	Periode
peu a peu, graduellement	allmählich, gradweisse
phrase	Phrase
phrasé	Phrasierung
pieusement	andächtig
pincé	Schneller, Praller
pincer	zupfen, anreissen
pizzicato	gezupft
placide	ruhig, sanft
plaintif, triste	klagend, gemendo
plaisant, charmant	gefällig, angenehm
plateau	Plattenteller
plein	volltsnig, rund
pleurant	weinand
plus	mehr
podium	Podium
point, pointé	Punkt, punktiert

ITALIAN	ENGLISH
partitura, spartito	score
passaggio	transition
appassionato	passionately
pastorale	pastoral
patetico	pathetic
penetrante, acuto	penetrating, shrill
frase, periodo	period [form]
poco a poco	little by little, gradually
frase	phrase
articolazione	phrasing
devoto	devoutedly
mordente superiore	inverted mordent
pizzicare, strappare	pluck (to)
pizzicato	plucked
pacato	placid
flebile	mournful, plaintive
piacevole, gradito	pleasing
piatto portadischi	turntable
pieno	full [as in full voice]
piangendo	weeping
più	more
podio	podium, rostrum
punto, puntato	dot, dotted

FRENCH	*GERMAN*
point d'orgue, pause, fermata	Halt, Fermate
pointe	Spitze
polonaise	Polonaise
polyphonique	polyphon
polythématique	vielthemig
pompeux	pompös
portamento	portamento
portée	Liniensystem
posément	bequem
position	Lage
postlude	Nachspiel
poussé	Hinstrich
précipité	überstürzt
précis, exact	genau
préparation	Vorbereitung
pressant, en	drängend
profane	weltlich
progression	Fortschreitung
prolongement	Tastenfessel
prolonger	aushalten
promptement	pronto, schnell
psaume	Psalm
puissant, fort	mächtig

ITALIAN	ENGLISH
fermata, corona	hold, fermata, pause
punta	tip, point
polacca	polonaise
polifono	polyphonic
politematico	polythematic
pomposo	pompous
portamento	scooping, carrying over
pentagramma	staff, stave
agiato	sedately
posizione	spacing [of a chord]
postludio	epilogue
arco in su	up bow
precipitato	precipitately
giusto	exact
preparazione	preparation
stringendo	quickening, urging on
profano	secular
progressione	progression
prolungamento	sustaining pedal
mantenere	sustain (to)
pronto	promptly
salmo	psalm
possènte, potente	mighty, powerful

FRENCH	*GERMAN*
pupitre	Notenpult, Pult
quarte	Quart
quartolet	Quartole
quatuor	Quartett
queue de la note	Notenhals
quinte	Quint
quintette	Quintett
quintolet	Quintole
ralentir	nachlassen
ralentissant, étendre	zuruckhaltend, langsamer werdend
rapide, rapidement	rasch, geschwind
réaliser	aussetzen
recenser	rezensieren
récitant	Testo
récitatif	Rezitativ
réciter	rezitieren
refrain	Wiederholung, Refrain
régie	Regie
régisseur	Spielleiter
registre	Stimmumfang
régler	regulieren
régulié, sans hâte	bedächtig
renforçant, en	mit starken Ton

ITALIAN	ENGLISH
leggio	stand, desk
quarta	fourth [interval]
quartina	quadruplet
quartetto	quartet
gambo della note	stem [of a note]
quinta	fifth [interval]
quintetto	quintet
quintina	quintuplet
rallentare	slow down (to)
ritardando, raffrenando, rallentando	slowing down
rapidissim, celere	rapidly, swiftly
realizzare	realize (to)
recensire	review, criticize (to)
testo	narrator
recitativo	recitative
recitare	recite (to)
ritornello	chorus, refrain
regia	production, stage direction
regista	producer, artistic director
estensione vocale	range [vocal]
regolare	regulate (to)
deliberatamente	unhurried
sforzando, sforzato	forcing, accenting

FRENCH	*GERMAN*
renforcé	verstärkt
répétition	Probe
répétition générale	Hauptprobe
répetiteur	Korrepetitor
réponse	Antwort, Riposta
représenter	aufführen
reprise	Wiederholung
reproduction	Nachdruck
Requiem, messe funèbre	Totenmesse
résonance	Nachklingen
résonnant	resonanzföhig
résoudre	auflösen
respiration	Luftpause
respirer	einatmen
retard	Vorhalt
retarder	nachhinken
retenu	züruckhaltend
retoucher	überarbeiten
rétrograde	krebsgängig
revenir	wiederkehren
réverbération	Nachhall
révision	Revision
ricercar	Ricercar
rigide, tendu	straff

ITALIAN	*ENGLISH*
rinforzato	reinforced, strengthened
prova	rehearsal
proba generale	dress rehearsal
ripetore	coach
risposta	answer, consequent
rappresentare	perform (to)
ripetizione	repetition
ristampa	reprint
requiem, messa funebre	Mass for the dead
risonanza	echo, resonance
risonante	resonant
risolvere	resolve (to)
respiro	breathing pause
inspirare	inhale (to)
ritardo	suspension
restare indietro	lag behind (to)
ritenuto	held back
rielaborare	rework (to), revise (to)
retrogrado	retrograde, crabwise
ricorrere	recur (to), return (to)
riverberazione	reverberation
revisione	revision
ricercare	ricercare
rigido, teso	tense, rigid, taut

FRENCH	*GERMAN*
rigoureux	streng [in Takt]
rinforzando	stärker werdend
rond, plein	rund
rubato	rubato
rythme	Rhythmus
sanglotant	schluchzend
sans	ohne
saut	Sprung
sauter	höpsen
sautillé	Springbogen
scander	skandieren
scénario	Drehbuch, Szenarium
sec, seche	trocken, kurz
seconde	Sekunnde
secouer, agiter	schütteln
section, parte	Teil
semi-brève	Semibrevis
septième	Septime
septuor	Septett
séquence	Folge
sérénade	Ständchen
série	Reihe
sérieux	ernst
seul	allein

ITALIAN	*ENGLISH*
rigoroso	strictly [in time]
rinforzando	strengthening
pieno, ampio	rounded, rich
rubato	robbed rhythm
ritmo	rhythm
singhiozzando	sobbing
senza	without
taglio	leap, skip
saltellare	hop, leap (to)
saltellato	bouncing [bow]
scandire	scan
scenario	scenario
secco	dry
seconda	second [interval]
scuotere, agitere	shake (to)
sezione, parte	section, part
semibrevis	whole note
settima	seventh [interval]
settimino	septet
seguito	sequence
serenata	serenade
serie	row, series
serioso	serious
solo	alone, solo

FRENCH	*GERMAN*
s'évanouir	abklingen
sévère	sttreng
sextolet	Sextole
sextuor	Sextett
siffler	pfeifen
signature	Signatur
signe	Zeichen
signe de la mesure	Taktvorzeichen
signe de reprise	Wiederholungszeichen
silence, pause	Pause
similaire	ebenfalls
simplement	einfach
sixte	Sexte
solennellement	feierlich
solfège	Solfeggio
sombre, triste	düster
son	Klang, Schall
son continu	Dauerton
sonate	Sonate
sonate de chambre	Kammersonate
sonate d'église	Kirchensonate
sonner	erklingen
sonore	klangvoll
souffle	Atem

ITALIAN	ENGLISH
morendo, sforzarsi	fade out, die away
severo, rigoroso	strict
sestina	sextuplet
sestetto	sextet
fischiare	whistle (to)
segnatura	signature
segno	mark, sign
segno di mesura	time signature
segno di ripetizione	repeat sign
pausa	rest
simile	similar, in a like manner
semplice	simply
sesta	sixth [interval]
solenne	solemnly
solfeggio	solfeggio
tetro, cupo	gloomy, dismal
suono	tone, sound
suono continuo	continuous tone
sonata	sonata
sonata da camera	chamber sonata
sonata da chiesa	church sonata
suonare	sound (to)
armonioso	harmonious
fiato	breath

FRENCH	GERMAN
souffleur	Souffleur
soupir	Seufzer
source	Quelle
sourd	kurzatmig
sourdine	Dämpfer
soutenir	stützen
spirituel	geistlich
sprechgesang	Sprechgesang
strette	Engführung
strophe	Strophe
structure	Struktur
style, écriture	Satzart
subitement	plötzlich
sublimité	Erhabenheit
successivement	hintereinander
suivre, enchaînez	folgen
sujet	Thema
syllabe	Silbe
syllabique	syllabisch
sympathetique	mitklingend
symphonie	Symphonie
syncope	Synkopierung
tablature	Griffnotation
tablature	Intabulierung

ITALIAN	ENGLISH
suggeritore	prompter
sospiro	sigh
fonte	origin, source
sordo	dull [in tone]
sordino	mute
sostenare	support (to)
spirituale	spiritual, sacred
canto-parlato	speech-song, inflected speech
stretto	stretto
strofa	stanza
struttura	structure
stile, scrittura	setting, style
subito	suddenly
elevatezza	sublimity
successivamente	seccessively
segue	continue [without break]
soggetto	subject, theme
sillaba	syllable
sillabico	syllablic
simpatico	sympathetic
sinfonia	symphony
sincope	syncopation
tablatura	tablature
intavolatura	intabulation

FRENCH	*GERMAN*
tapoter	klimpern
temps	Zeitmass
tendrement	liebvoll
ténor	Tenor
tension	Spannung
tenu, soutenu	gehalten, getragen
tenue	Bindung
tête de la note	Notenkopf
thématique	thematisch
théorique	theoretisch
tierce	Terz
timbre	Tonfarbe
tinter	bimmeln
tirage	Auflage
tiré	Herstrich
ton entier	Ganzton
tonal	tonlich
tonalité	Tonalität, Tonart
tonique	Tonikat
touche	Taste
tournez [la page!]	umblättern!
tous	alle
traînant	schleppend
transcription	übertragung

ITALIAN	*ENGLISH*
strimpellare	strum (to)
tempo	tempo, speed
amoroso	tenderly
tenore	tenor
tensione	tension
sostenuto, tenendo	sustained
legatura	tie, slur
testina	notehead
tematico	thematic
teorico, teoretico	theoretical
terza	third [interval]
timbro	tone color
tintinnare	tinkle (to)
edizione	issue, edition
arco in giu	down bow
tono [intero]	whole tone
tonale	tonal
tonalità, tono	key, mode, tonality,
tonica	tonic
tasto	note, key
volti!	turn [the page!]
tutti	all
trascinando, stentando	dragging
trascrizione	transcription

FRENCH	*GERMAN*
transposer	transponieren
tremblant	zitternd
trille	Triller
trio	Terzett
triolet	Triole
trop	zu sehr
tsigane	Zigeuner
unisson	Einklang, Prim
vague	unbestimmt
valeur de la note	Notenwert
vélocité	Geläufigkeit
velouté	samtig
version	Fassung
verve, élan	Schmiss
vibrato	Bebung
vibrer	schwingen, vibrieren
vif, agilement	behende
villageois	bauernlich
virtuose	virtuos
virtuosité	Kunstfertigkeit
vite, rapide	schnell
vivement	lebendig, lebhaft
vocalise	Vokalise
voilé, brumeux	verschliert

ITALIAN	ENGLISH
traspotare	transpose (to)
tremolando	trembling
trillo	trill, shake
terzetto	trio
terzina	triplet
troppo	too much
zingaro	gypsy
unisono	unison
vago	vague
valore della note	note value
scorrevolezza	velocity
vellutato	velvety
versione	version
brio	verve
vibrato	vibrato
vibrare	vibrate (to)
svelto	agile, nimbly
contadinesco	rustic, country-like
virtuoso	masterly, virtuoso
virtuosità	virtuosity
presto	fast
vivo	lively
vocalizzo	vocalise
velato	veiled, husky [voice]

FRENCH	*GERMAN*
voix, partie	Stimme
volant	fliegend
zèle	zele, eifger

ITALIAN	*ENGLISH*
parte, voce	voice, part
volante	rushing
zelo	zeal

GERMAN

GERMAN	ITALIAN
abbrechen	troncare
Abendlied, Nocturne	notturno
abgemessen	misurato, a battuta
abgestossen	staccato
abgezetzt	scucito
abklingen	smorzarsi
abnehmend, leiser werdend	dimenuendo, scemando
Abschluss	coda
abschwellen	diminuire
absetzen	articolare
absteigen	descendere, abbassare
abtaktig	in battere
abwärts	discendente
abwechselnd	alternando
Achtelnote	croma
ad libitum, belieben	a libito, beneplacito
adagietto	adagietto
ängstlich	affannato
antwort, riposta	riposta
agitirt, erregt	concitato
akkord	accordo
Akustik	acustica
alle	tutti
allein	solo

FRENCH	ENGLISH
arrêter	break off
nocturne	nocturne
mesure, à la mesure	strict time, measured
détaché	detached
détaché	unconnected, non legato
s'évanouir	fade out, die away
diminuendo, en diminuant	dying away, getting softer
coda	coda
diminuer	decrease (to) [dynamics]
articuler	separate (to), articulate (to)
descendre, abaisser	descend, lower
frappé	downbeat
descendant	downward
changeant, en	alternating
croche	eighth-note
à volanté	freely
adagietto	adagietto, faster than adagio
angoissé	anguished
réponse	answer, consequent
excité, animé	excited, stirred
accord	chord
acoustique	acoustics, science of sound
tous	all
seul	alone

GERMAN	ITALIAN
allmählich, gradweisse	poco a poco
andächtig	devoto
andante, gehend	andante
Andeutung	indicato
Anfang, Eintretend	cominciare
Anfang [von]	da capo, dal segno
angenehm, gefüllig	piacevole, gradito
angstvoll	pauroso
animoso, beherzt	animoso, animosamente
anmuthig, graziös	grazioso
Ansatz, Mondloch	imboccatura
anschwellen	addensare, ispessire
anspielen, einsatzen	attaccare
Antwort	risposta
arpeggiert, gebrochen	arpeggiando, arpeggiato
artikulieren	granire
Atem	fiato, respiro
aufführen	rappresentare
aufhalten	poggiato
auflösen	risolvere
Aufnahme	registrazione
Auftakt	anacrusi
aufwärtsgehend	salendo
ausatmen	espirare

FRENCH	ENGLISH
peu a peu, graduellement	little by little, gradually
pieusement	devoutedly
andante, allant	walking , moderately
indicatif	indication
commencement	beginning
depuis le commencement	repeat from the beginning
plaisant, agréable	pleasing, agreeably
craintif, timide	timidly
animé, hardiment	spirited, resolutely
aimable, gracieux	gracefully
embouchure	embouchure
augmenter	grow louder
attaquer	attack (to)
réponse	answer, consequence
arpégé	broken, arpeggiated
détacher	articulate (to)
souffle	breath
représenter	perform (to)
appuyer	leaned upon
résoudre	resolve (to)
enregistrement	recording
anacrouse	upbeat
ascendant	ascending, upwards
expirer	exhale

GERMAN	*ITALIAN*
ausdrucksvoll	espressivo
Ausführung	esecuzione
bald, schnell	tosto
barsch, heftig	brusco, bruscamente
Batterie	batteria
bauernlich	contadinesco
bearbeiten	trascrivere
Bebung	vibrato
bedächtig	deliberatamente
bedrohlich, drohend	minacciosamente
begeisterung	ispirazione
begleiten	accompagnare
behende	svelto
beherzt, kühn	audace
belebt	animato
beruhingend	calmando
beschleunigung	ravvivando
bestimmt, deutlich	distinto, chiaro
bestimmt, entschieden	deciso, decisamente
betont	accentato
betrübt, schmerz	addolorato
beweglichkeit	lestezza
bewegt	agitato
bewegt	mosso

FRENCH	ENGLISH
expressivo	expressively
exécution	performance
bientôt, vite	soon, quick
brusque, brusquement	brusquely, abruptly
batterie	percussion section
villageois	rustic, country-like
arranger	arrange (to)
vibrato	vibrato
régulié	unhurried
minacciosamente	threateningly
inspiration, enthousiasme	inspiration, enthusiasm
accompagner	accompany (to)
vif, agilement	agile, nimbly
audace, audacieux	audacious, bold
animé	brisk, animated
calmant	calming
pressant	quicken
nettement, distinctement	distinct,clear
décidé, avec résolution	resolutely, decisively
accentué, appuyé	accented, stressed
douleur, douloureaux	grief, sadness
agilité	agility, quickness
agité	agitated
mosso	moving, animated

GERMAN	ITALIAN
Bewegung	moto
bimmeln	tintinnare
Bindeklappe	legatura
Bindung	tenuto
bis	al
bravour, beherzt	bravura
brillant, glänzend	brillante
brummen	brontolare
brummstimmen	bocca chiusa
Chor	coro
Couplet	episodio
Dämpfer	sordino
Deklamation, Rezitativ	declamazione
demanchieren	smanicare
demütig	sommesso
detonieren	stonare
deutlich, klar	chiaro, nettamente
diatonisch	diatonico
dirigieren	dirigere
Diskordanz	discordia
Dissonanz	dissonanza
Divertimento	divertimento
doppelt	doppio
Doppelzunge	doppio colpo di lingua

FRENCH	ENGLISH
mouvement	motion, movement
tinter	tinkle (to)
ligature	slur
tenue	tie
à	to
bravoure, courage	bravura, courage
brillant	brilliant
bourdonner	hum (to)
bouche fermé	humming [with closed mouth]
choeur	chorus, choir
couplet	episode
sourdine	mute
déclamation	declamation, recitative
démancher	shift [position]
voilé	weak [voice]
détonner	waver in pitch, sing off pitch
net, clair	clear, distinct
diatonique	diatonic
diriger	conduct (to)
désaccordé	discordant, out of tune
dissonant	dissonance
divertissement	divertisement
double	doubled
double articulation	double tonguing

GERMAN	ITALIAN
dramatisch	drammatico
drängend	stringendo
Drehbuch, Szenarium	copione
Dreiklang	triade
Druck	stampa
dünn	esile
durchdringend	pentrante, acuto
Dürchführung	sviluppo, svolgimento
Durchgang	passaggio
düster	tetro, cupo
ebenfalls	simile
edel	nobile
eifrig	acceso
eilen, hastig, triebend	sollecitando
einatmen	inspirare
einfach	semplice
Einklang, Prim	unisono
Einsatz	entrée
einschieben	interpolare
Einschnitt	cesura
einspielen	registrare
einstimmen	accordare
Ende	fine
endlich	ultimo

FRENCH	ENGLISH
dramatique	dramatic
pressant	quickening, urging on
scénario	scenario
triade	triad
iompression	print, edition
fin	thin, reedy
pénétrant	penetrating, shrill
développement	development [thematic]
passage	transition
sombre, triste	gloomy, dismal
similaire	similar, in a like manner
noblement	noble, grand
acceso	fiery
empressé, hâter	hastening, pressing
respirer	inhale (to)
simplement	simply
unisson	unison
empressé, hâter	cue, entry
insérer	interpolate (to)
é sure	caesura, cut
enregistrer	record (to)
accorder	tune up (to)
fin	end
dernier	last, ultimate

GERMAN	ITALIAN
Endung	cadenza
Engführung	stretto
enharmonisch	enarmonico
enorm, riesig	tremendo
entfernt	lontano
Enthusiasmus	entusiasmo
Entlehnung	prestito
entspannen	distendire
Entwurf	abbozzo
erhaben	esaltare
eröhen	alzare
erklingen	suonare
erniedrigen	abbassare, bemollizzare
Erniedrigunszeichen	bemolle
ernst	serioso
erreichen	avvicinare
Ersatzspieler	sostituto
erweitern	allargare
Exequien	esequies
falsch	falsa
Falsett	falsetto
Fantasie	fantasia
fantasieren	improvvisare
Fassung	versione

FRENCH	ENGLISH
terminaison	cadence
strette	stretto
enharmonique	enharmonic
terrible	tremendous
éloigné	remote
enthousiasme	enthusiasm
emprunt	borrowing
détendre	relax (to)
détente	draft, sketch
célébrer	extol, praise
hausser	raise (to), sharpen
sonner	sound (to)
baisser	lower, flatten
bémol	flat [sign]
sérieux	serious
approcher, atteindre	approach, reach (to)
doublure	understudy
élargir	expand, extend
obsèques	obsequies
faux	false
fausset	falsetto [voice]
fantaisie	fantasia
improviser	improvise (to)
version	version

GERMAN	ITALIAN
Fauxbourdon	falso bordone
feierlich	solenne
Fertigkeit	abilità
fest	fermo
festlich, freudig	festoso, festivo
feurig	acceso, focoso
fiero, stolz	fiero, fieramente
figurieren	figurare
Filz	feltro
Fingersatz	diteggiatura
Flatterzunge	frullato
fliegend	volante
fliessend	scorrendo, scorrevole
flottant	flottuante
Folge	seguito
folgen	segue
forcieren	forzare, rinforzare
forte, laut	forte
frei	libero
frenetico, rasend	frenetico
Frequenz	frequenza
friedlich	placido
frisch	fresco
frivol	frivolo

FRENCH	ENGLISH
faux-bourdon	fauxbourdon
solennel	solemnly
dexterité	dexterity
ferme	firmly
joyeux, festivo	merry, festive
acceso, avec fougue	fiery
fuer, fiêrement	proudly, fiercely
orner, figurer	ornament (to), embellish (to)
feutre	felt
doigté	fingering
articulation double	flutter-tonguing
volant	rushing
coulant, facile	flowing, fluid
flottant	floating
séquence	progression
suivre, enchaînez	continue [without break]
forcer	force, push [the sound]
forte, à haut voix	loud, strong
libre	free
frénetique	madly, frenetically
fréquence	frequency
placide	placid
fraichement	freshly
frivole	frivolous

GERMAN	ITALIAN
fröhlich, lebhaft	gioioso
froh	lieto
funkelnd	scintillante
Gage	onorario
Galopp	galop, galoppo
Ganzton	tono [intero]
Garn	filo
Gattung	specie
gebunden	legato
gedeckt	scurito
gefällig, angenehm	piacevole, gradito
gefühlvoll	molto sentimento (con)
Gegenbewegung	moto contrario
Gegenmelodie	controcanto
Gegensatz	controsoggetto
gehalten, getragen	sostenuto, tenendo
geheimnisvoll	misterioso
geistlich	spirituale
Geklimper	strimpello
gelassen, beruhigend	calmato
Geläufigkeit	scorrevolezza
gemächlich,	comodo
gemendo	gemendo

FRENCH	ENGLISH
joyeux, gai	joyous
aisé	glad, joyous
brillant	sparkling
cachet	fee
galop	gallop
ton entier	whole tone
fil	thread
espèce	species
lié	slurred, tied
couvert, voilé	muffled [voice]
plaisant, charmant	pleasing
beaucoup de sentiment (avec)	full of feeling
mouvement contraire	contrary motion
contre-thème	counter-melody
contre-sujet	countersubject
tenu, soutenu	sustained
mystérieusement	mysteriously
spirituel	spiritual, sacred
tapotage	strumming
tranquille, calme	calm, calmly
vèlocitè	velocity
commodément	comfortable, leisurely
plaintif	lamenting

GERMAN	*ITALIAN*
genau	giusto
Geräusch	rumore
gesanglich, singend	cantabile, cantando
geschmackvoll	gusto [con]
gestopft	chiuso
geteilt	divisi
gewiss	risoluto
gezupft	pizzicato
Glanz	lustro
gleichgültigkeit	negligente
gleichmässig	equabile, uniforme
gleitend	glissando
Grabgesang, Todeslied	canto funebre
Griffnotation	tablatura
grossartig	maestoso
hämmernd	martellato
Härte	durezza, asprezza
Halbton	semitono
Halt, Fermate	fermata, corona
hauchig	soffiato
heftig, stürmish	impetuoso
heroisch	eroico
Herstrich	arco in giu
Hilfslinie	taglio linea supplementare

FRENCH	ENGLISH
précis, exact	exact
bruit	noise
chantant	melodiously, singing
goét [avec]	stylishly
étouffé	stopped [horn]
divisé	divided
décidé, décisif	bold, determined
pincé	plucked
éclat	brilliance
insouciant	carelessly, with indifference
égal	even, equal
glissando, en glissant	glissando, sliding
chant funèbre	dirge, funeral song
tablature	tablature
grand	grand, great
martelé	hammered
dureté	harshness
demi-ton	semitone, half tone
point d'orgue	hold, fermata
murmuré	breathy
précipité	impetuous
héroique	heroic
tiré	down bow
ligne supplémentaire	ledger line

GERMAN	ITALIAN
hinsterbend, ersterbend	morendo, mancando
Hinstrich	arco in su
hintereinander	successivamente
hitzig	di fuoco
hoch	alto, acuto
höfisch	cortigianesco
Höhe	altezza
höpsen	saltellare
hörbar	udibile
hören	udire, ascoltare
hurtig, leicht	snèllo
im Tact, im Zeitmas	a tempo
imperfekt	imperfetto
imponierend	imponente
impuls, Stosskraft	slancio
inbrünstig	fervido
innig	sentito
inständig	insistamente
instrumentieren	strumentare
Intabulierung	intavolatura
interpretieren	interpretare
Intonation	intonazione
intonieren	intonare
ironisch	ironico

FRENCH	ENGLISH
diminuer, éteindre	dying away
poussé	up bow
successivement	successively
fougueux	hot, fiery, impetuous
haut, aigu	high
de cour	courtly
hauteur	upper notes, treble
sauter	hop, leap (to)
perceptible	audible
entendre, écouter	hear (to)
légér, agilement	nimble, agile
en measure	in tempo
imparfait	imperfect
imposant	imposing in style
impulsion, vitesse	impetus, outburst
ardemment	fervently
intime	heartfelt
insistence [avec]	urgently
instrumenter	orchestrate (to)
tablature	intabulation
interpréter	interpretation
intonation	intonation
entonner	intone (to)
ironiquement	ironical

GERMAN	ITALIAN
jovialisch	gioioso
jubelnd	giubbilose
kadenzierend	cadenzale
Kammersonate	sonata da camera
Kenner	intenditore
Kirchensonata	sonata da chiesa
klagend	flebile
Klang, Schall	suono
klangvoll	armonioso
Klaviatur	tastiera
kleben	congiungere
klimpern	strimpellare
komisch	buffo
Kontrapunkt	contrappunto
korrepetieren	provare
kosend, schmeichelnd	carezzando
krebsgängig	retrogrado
Kreis	ciclo
kriegerisch	marziale
kühn, keck	ardito, arditamente
Kunstfertigkeit	virtuosità
kurzatmig	sordo
lärmend	strepitoso

FRENCH	ENGLISH
joyeux, plaisant	merrily, cheerful
jubilant	jubilant
cadentiel	cadencing
sonata de chambre	chamber sonata
connaisseur	connoisseur
sonate d'église	church sonata
plaintif, triste	mournful, plaintive
son	tone, sound
sonore	harmonious
clavier	keyboard
coller	splice (to)
tapoter	strum (to)
comique	comical
contrepoint	counterpoint
entrainer	coach (to)
caressant	caressing, flattering
rétrograde	retrograde, crabwise
cycle	cycle, circle
martial	martial
audacieux, hardi	bold, courageous
virtuosité	virtuosity
sourd	dull [in tone]
bruyant	noisy

GERMAN	ITALIAN
Lage	posizione
langsam	tardo, tardamento
Laufzeit	durata
launenhaft	capriccioso
launig	umore
lauter werdend	crescendo
lebendig, lebhaft	vivo
leicht	leggiero
leidenschaftlich	appassionato
leise	piano
leiser werdend	decrescendo
Lied	canzone
Linie	linea
Liniensystem	pentagramma
Lobegesang	inno
loslassen	abbandonare
Luftpause	respiro
mächtig	possènte, potente
magnifico, prächtig	magnifico
majestätisch	maestoso
Manieren	abbellimenti
markiert	marcato
Marsch	marcia
mehr	più

FRENCH	ENGLISH
position	spacing [of a chord]
lent	slow
duré	duration, playing time
capricieux	capricious
plaisant	humor
crescendo	louder gradually
vivement	lively
facile	lightly
passionné	passionately
doux	soft
en diminuant	softer, gradually
mélodie	song
ligne	line [of a staff]
portée	staff, stave
chanson laudative	hymn [of praise]
lácher	release (to)
respiration	breathing pause
puissant, fort	mighty, powerful
magnifique	magnificent
majestueux	majestic
ornements	ornaments
marqué	marked, accented
marche	march
plus	more

GERMAN	ITALIAN
Melodram	melodramma
Merkmal	caratteristica
militärisch	militare
mischen	fondere
mit	con, col, colla
mitklingend	simpatico
Mitleid	pieta, pietoso
mitsingen	cantare insieme
Modell, Vorlage	modello
Modulation	modulazione
Moll	minore
Mordent	mordente
Motette	motetto
Motiv	motivo
müde, erschlaffen	languendo
murmelnd, gehaucht	mormorando
Nachahmung	imitazione
nachdrücklich	enfatico
Nachdruck	ristampa
nachgebend	cedendo
Nachhall	riverberazione
nachhinken	restare indietro
Nachklingen	risonanza

FRENCH	*ENGLISH*
mélodrame	melodrama
caractéristque	characteristic, feature
militaire	military
mélanger	blend (to)
avec	with
sympathetique	sympathetic
dolent	pity, mercy
chanter avec	sing with (to)
modèle	pattern, model
modulation	modulation
mineur	minor [mode]
mordant	mordant [ornament]
motet	motet
motif	motive
langueur	languishing
murmurant	whispering, murmuring
imitation	imitation
emphatique	emphatically
reproduction	reprint
en cédent	holding back
réverbération	reverberation
retarder	lag behind (to)
résonance	echo, resonance

GERMAN	ITALIAN
nachlassen	rallentare
Nachspiel	postludio
nichttonal	non tonale
niederdrücken	abbassare
None	nona
Nonett	nonetto
Normalton	diapason
Notenbalken	tratto d'unione
Notenfahne	codetta
Notenhals	gambo della note
Notenpapier	carta da musica
Notenpult, Notenständer	leggio
Notenwert	valore della note
Oberton	armonico
obligat	obbligato
oder	ossia
ohne	senza
Ohr	orecchio
Oktett	ottetto
Particell	particella
Partitur, Sparte	partitura, spartito
Pastorale, Hirtenlied	pastorale
pathetisch	patètico
Pause	pausa

FRENCH	ENGLISH
ralentir	slow down (to)
postlude	epilogue
atonal	non-tonal
abaisser	depress (to)
neuvième	ninth
nonet	nonet
diapason standard	standard pitch
barre transversale	beam, cross-bar
crochet de la note	tail, flag [of a note]
queue de la note	stem [of a note]
papier à musique	manuscript paper
pupitre	music stand
valeur de la note	note value
harmonique	overtone
obligé	obligatory
ou	or
sans	without
oreille	ear
octuor	octet
partie	short score
partition	score
pastorale	pastoral
pathétique	pathetic
silence, pause	rest

GERMAN	ITALIAN
Periode	frase, periodo
pfeifen	fischiare
Pfundnote	nota tenuta
Phrasieruing	articolazione
Plattenteller	piatto portadischi
plötzlich, sofort	subito
Podium	podio
Polonaise	polacca
pompös	pomposo
Primgeige	primo violino
Probe	prova
Proposta, Leitmelodie	proposta
Psalm	salmo
Punkt, punktiert	punto, puntato
Quadratnotation	notazione quadrata
Quart	quarta
Quartett	quartetto
Quartole	quartina
Quelle	fonte
Quint	quinta
quintenrein	quinte giuste
Quintett	quintetto
Quintole	quintina
rasch	rapidissimo

FRENCH	ENGLISH
partie, période	period [form]
siffler	whistle (to)
note tenue	long note
phrasé	phrasing
plateau	turntable
subitement	suddenly
podium	podium, rostrum
polanaise	polonaise
pompeux	pompous
premier violon	first violin
répétition	rehearsal
antécédent	antecedent [canon]
psaume	psalm
point, pointé	dot, dotted
notation carée	square notation
quarte	fourth [interval]
quatuor	quartet
quartolet	quadruplet
source	origin, source
quinte	fifth [interval]
quintes justes	perfect fifths [in]
quintette	quintet
quintolet	quintuplet
rapidement	rapidly

GERMAN	ITALIAN
rauh, hart-klingend	aspramente
redend, sprechen	parlando, parlante
reduzieren	ridotto
Refrain	ritornello
Regie	regia
regulieren	regolare
rein	giusto
resonanzföhig	risonante
revidieren	rivedare
rezensieren	recensire
Rezitativ	recitativo
rezitieren	recitare
Rhythmus	ritmo
Ricercar	ricercare
ritenuto	ritenuto
Rohrblatt	ancia
rubato	rubato
ruhelos, unheimlich	inquietante
ruhig, sanft	pacato
rund	ampio
Sänger	cantante
Saite	corda
Sammlung	raccolta
samtig	vellutato

FRENCH	ENGLISH
aigrement, âpre	harshly
parler	speaking
réduire	reduced, arranged
refrain	refrain, chorus
régie	production, stage direction
régler	regulate
juste, parfait	perfect [interval]
résonnant	resonant
réviser	revise (to)
recenser	review, criticize (to)
récitatif	recitative
réciter	recite (to)
rythme	rhythm
ricercar	ricercare
retenu	held back
anche	reed
rubato	robbed rhythm
inquiet, agité	restless, uneasy
placide	placid
rond, plein	rounded, rich
chanteur	singer, vocalist
corde	string
collection	collection
velouté	velvety

GERMAN	ITALIAN
sanft	soave
Satz	movimento
Satzart	stile, scrittura
schaffen	creare
schalkhaft	malignamente
Schall	suono
schalldicht	isolante
schallhart	riverberante
Schallplatte	disco
schallweich	assorbente
schauerlich	macabro
scherzhaft	scherzando
Schlag, Schwebung	battito
schleppend	trascinando, stentando
schluchzend	singhiozzando
Schlüssel	chiave
Schluss, Endung	cadenza, chiusa
schmachtend	languido
schmerzhaft	dolente, dolore
schmerzlich	doloroso
Schmiss	brio
schnell	presto
Schneller, Praller	mordente superiore
schreiend	stridento, strillo

FRENCH	ENGLISH
doucement	gently, suavely
mouvement	movement [of a work]
style, écriture	harmony, setting, style
créer	create (to)
espièglement	roguishly
son	sound
insonorisé	soundproof
dur	hard
disque	disc, recording
mou	soft [texture]
macabre	macabre
badinant	joking
battement	beat
traînant	dragging
pleurant	sobbing
clef, clé	clef
cadence, terminaison	cadence, close
languissant	languidly
dolent, triste	sorrowful, pathetic
douloureaux	sad, painful
verve, élan	verve
vite, rapide	fast
pincé	inverted mordent
strident	sharp, shrill

GERMAN	ITALIAN
Schritt	grado
schrittweise	congiunto, di grado
schütteln	scuotere, agitere
schwach	fiacca, debole
schwächer	indebolendo
schwankend	barcollante
schwer	grave, pesante
Schwerpunkt	enfasi
schwingen, vibrieren	vibrare
Sechzehntelnote	semicroma
Seitenbewegung	moto obliquo
sehr	assai
Semibrevis, Ganze	semibrevis
Septett	settimino
Sequenz	sequenza
Seufzer	sospiro
Sexte	sesta
Sextett	sestetto
Sextole	sestina
Signatur	segnatura
Silbe	sillaba
Singmanieren	abbellimenti vocali
skandieren	scandire
Solfeggio	solfeggio

FRENCH	ENGLISH
degré	step
par degrés conjoints	stepwise
secouer, agiter	shake (to)
faible	feeble
affaiblissant	weaken
oscillant	swaying
lent, avec gravité	solemn, heavy, slow
accent	stress
vibrer	vibrate (to)
double croche	sixteenth-note
mouvement oblique	oblique motion
beaucoup, très	very
semi-brève	whole note
septuor	septet
séquence	sequence
soupir	sigh
sixte	sixth
sextuor	sextet
sextolet	sextuplet
signature	signature
syllabe	syllable
broderies	vocal ornaments
scander	scan
solfège	solfeggio

GERMAN	ITALIAN
Sonate	sonata
Souffleur	suggeritore
Spannung	tensione
spasshaft	giocoso
Spiegelfuge	fuga a specchio
Spielart	tocco
spielen	suonare
Spielleiter	regista
Spielmann	menestrello
Spitze	punta
Sprechgesang	canto-parlato
Sprechmelodie	inflessione della voce
Springbogen	spiccato
Sprung	taglio
Ständchen	serenata
stärker werdend	rinforzando
starken akzentuiertem	sforzando, sforzato
Steg	ponticello
steigern	intensificare
Stichwort	chiamata
Stillstand	arresto
Stimme	parte, voce
Stimmfall	inflessione

FRENCH	*ENGLISH*
sonate	sonata
souffleur	prompter
tension	tension
joyeux	merry, jocular
fugue en miroir	mirror fugue
attaque	touch
jouer	play (to)
régisseur	producer, artistic director
ménestrel	minstrel
pointe	tip, point
sprechgesang	speech-song, inflected speech
inflexion de la voix	vocal inflection, speech-melody
sautillé	bouncing [bow]
saut	leap, skip
sérénade	serenade
renforcent	strengthening
renforçant	forced, accented
chevalet	bridge
intensifier	intensify (to)
réplique	cue
arrêt, silence	stop
voix, partie	voice, part
inflexion	inflection

GERMAN	*ITALIAN*
Stimmung	stato d'animo
Stimmumfang	estensione vocale
stolz	fiero, fieramente
straff	rigido, teso
streichen	suonare con l'arco
Streichung	taglio
streng	severo, rigoroso
Strophe	strofa
Struktur	struttura
stürmisch	tempestoso
stützen	sostenare
syllabisch	sillabico
Symphonie	sinfonia
Synkopierung	sincope
tänzerisch	di danza
Takt	misura
Taktschlagen	battere il tempo
Taktstock	bacchetta
Taktstrich	stanghetta
Taktvorzeichen	segno d'indicazione
Taktzahl	numero di battute
Taste	tasto
Tastenfessel	prolungamento
Teil	sezione, parte

FRENCH	ENGLISH
climat	mood
registre	range [vocal]
fier, fièrement	proudly, fiercely
rigide, tendu	tense, rigid, taut
jouer avec l'archet	bow (to)
coupure	cut
sévère	strict
strophe	stanza
structure	structure
orageux	tempestuous
soutenir	support (to)
syllabique	syllabic
symphonie	symphony
syncope	syncopation
dansant	dancing
mesure, tempo	bar, measure
battre la mesure	beat time (to)
baguette	baton
barre	barline
signe de la mesure	time signature
numéro de la mesure	bar number
touche	note, key
prolongement	sustaining pedal
section, partie	section, part

GERMAN	*ITALIAN*
Tenor	tenore
Terz	terza
Terzett	terzetto
Testo	testo
Textdichter	poeta
Textverfasser	librettista
Thema	soggetto
thematisch	tematico
theoretisch	teorico, teoretico
tief	basso, grave
Titelblatt	frontespizio
Tonalität	tonalità
Tonart	tono
Tonfarbe	timbro
Tonhöhe	altezza del suono
Tonika	tonica
Tonkunst	musica
Tonleiter	scala
tonlich	tonale
Tonsatz	composizione
Tonsilbenschrift	notazione sillabica
Totenmesse	requiem
trällern	cantarellare
transponieren	traspotare

FRENCH	ENGLISH
ténor	tenor
tierce	third
trio	trio
récitant	narrator
parolier, poète	poet, lyricist
auteur	author, librettist
sujet	subject, theme
thématique	thematic
théorique	theoretical
bas, profund	deep, low
page de titre	title page
tonalité	tonality
tonalité	key, mode, tonality
timbre	tone color
hauteur du son	pitch, pitch level
tonique	tonic
musique	music, tonal art
gamme, échelle	scale
tonal	tonal
composition	composition
notation syllabique	syllabic notation
Requiem, messe funèbre	Mass for the dead
fredonner	trill (to), warble (to)
transposer	transpose (to)

GERMAN	*ITALIAN*
traümerisch	trasognato
traurig, wehmütig	mesto, triste
Tremolo	tremolo
Triller	trillo
Triole	terzina
trocken, kurz	secco
tröstend	consolante
Tusch	fanfara
üben	esercitare
überarbeiten	rielaborare
Übertragung	trascripzione
umblättern!	volti!
Umdeutung	reinterpretazione
Umfang, Raum	estensione
Umkehrung	rivolto
Umspielung	parafrasi
unbestimmt	vago
unbetonnt	non accentato
Undezime	undicesima
unentschieden	irresoluto
ungeduldig	impazientemente
ungezwungen	disinvolto
unhörbar	inudibile
unruhig, heftig bewegt	irrequieto

FRENCH	ENGLISH
comme dans un songe	dreamily
douloureaux, triste	sad, mournful
trémolo	tremolo
trille	trill, shake
triolet	triplet
sec, seche	dry
consolant	consoling
fanfare, sonnerie	flourish, fanfare
exercise	exercise (to)
retoucher	rework (to), revise (to)
transcription	transcription
tournez [la page!]	turn [the page!]
équivoque	reintepretation
ambitus	range, compass
inversion	inversion
paraphrase	paraphrase
vague	vague
non accentué	unaccented
onzièame	eleventh [interval]
indécis	undecided [in style]
impatiemment	impatiently
alerte	easy going
inaudible	inaudible
inquiet, agité	nervous, restless

GERMAN	ITALIAN
Unterricht	istruzione
unvollständig	incompleto
unvorbereitet	non preparato
unzusammen-hüngend	incoerente
verhallend	sperdendosi (perdendosi)
verkleinern, diminuieren	diminuire
verkürzung	riduzione
Verleger	editore
verlöschend	estinguendo, mancando
verschliert	velato
verstärkt	rinforzato
verstimmt	scordato
verzweifelt	disperato
vielthemig	politematico
virtuos	virtuoso
Vocalise	vocalizzo
volltsnig, rund	pieno
von	di
Vorbereitung	preparazione
Vorhalt	ritardo
Vorsingen	audizione
Vorspiel	preludio
Vortrag	interpretazione
wackeln	tremolare

FRENCH	*ENGLISH*
enseignement	instruction, lesson
incomplet	incomplete
non préparé	unprepared
incohérent	incoherent, unconnected
en mourant	dying away
diminuer	diminish (to) {interval]
abbréviation	abbreviate (to), shorten (to)
éditeur	publisher
diminuant, éteindre	fading away
voilé, brumeux	veiled, husky [voice]
renforcé	reinforced, strengthened
désaccordé	out of tune
désesperé	desperately
polythématique	polythematic
virtuose	masterly, virtuoso
vocalise	vocalise
plein, pleine	full [as in full voice]
de	of
préparation	preparation
retard	suspension
audition	audition
ouverture	overture, prelude
interprétation	interpretation
chevroter	wobble (to)

GERMAN	ITALIAN
wegschaffen	levare
Weise, Melodik	melodia
weltlich	profano
wie	come
Wiederholung, Refrain	ritornello
Wiederholungszeichen	segni di ripetizione
wiederkehren	ricorrere
wild	feroce
wogend	ondeggiando
wohlklingend	eufonico
zählnen	contare
zart, süss	dolce, raddolcendo
Zeichen	segno
Zeitmass	tempo
zele, eifger	zelo
ziemlich	mezzo
zierlich	garbato
Ziffer	cifra
Zigeuner	zingaro
Zischlaut	sibilante
zitieren	citare
zitternd	tremolando
zögern	ritardare
zornig, erregt	adirato

FRENCH	ENGLISH
éloigner	to take off [remove]
air	tune, melody
profane	secular
comme	as
refrain	chorus, refrain
signe de reprise	repeat sign
revenir	recur (to), return (to)
féroce, sauvage	ferocious, wild
ondoyant	undulating, wavering
euphonie	euphonious
compter	count (to)
doucement, doux	sweetly, softly
signe	mark, sign
temps	meter
zèle	zeal
assez	fairly
gracieux	polite, graceful
chiffrage	figure
tsigane	gypsy
lettre sifflante	sibilant
citer	quote (to)
tremblant	trembling
hésiter	hesitate (to), retard (to)
colèrique	angered, irate

GERMAN	ITALIAN
zu sehr	troppo
Zugabe	bis
zuhören	ascoltare
zupfen, anreissen	pizzicare, strappare
zurückhaltend, langsamer werdend	ritardando, raffrendando, rallentando
zwei Gesang	a due

FRENCH	ENGLISH
trop	too much
encore	encore, again
écouter	listen (to)
pincer	pluck (to)
ralentissant, étendre	slowing down
à deux	two voices or instruments

ENGLISH

ENGLISH	*ITALIAN*
abbreviate (to), shorten (to)	riduzione
accented, stressed	accentato
accompany (to)	accompagnare
acoustics, science of sound	acustica
adagietto, faster than adagio	adagietto
agile, nimbly	svelto
agility, quickness	lestezza
agitated	agitato
all	tutti
alone	solo
alternating	alternando
angered, irate	adirato
anguished	affannato
answer, consequence	risposta
antecedent [canon]	proposta
approach, reach (to)	avvicinare
arrange (to)	trascrivere
articulate (to)	granire
as	come
ascending, upwards	salendo
attack (to)	attaccare
audacious, bold	audace
audible	udibile
audition	audizione

FRENCH	GERMAN
abbréviation	verkürzung
accentué, appuyé	betont
accompagner	begleiten
acoustique	Akustik
adagietto	adagietto
vif, agilement	behende
agilité	beweglichkeit
agité	bewegt
tous	alle
seul	allein
changeant, en	abwechselnd
colèrique	zornig, erregt
angoissé	ängstlich
réponse	Antwort, Riposta
antécédent	Proposta, Leitmelodie
approcher, atteindre	erreichen
arranger	bearbeiten
détacher	artikulieren
comme	wie
ascendant	aufwärtsgehend
attaquer	anspielen, einsatzen
audace, audacieux	beherzt, kühn
perceptible	hörbar
audition	Vorsingen

ENGLISH	*ITALIAN*
author, librettist	librettista
bar, measure	misura
bar number	numero di battute
barline	stanghetta
baton	bacchetta
beam, cross-bar	tratto d'unione
beat	battito
beat time (to)	battere il tempo
beginning	cominciare
blend (to)	fondere
bold, courageous	ardito, arditamente
borrowing	prestito
bouncing [bow]	spiccato
bow (to)	suonare con l'arco
bravura, courage	bravura
break off	troncare
breath	fiato, respiro
breathing pause	respiro
breathy	soffiato
bridge	ponticello
brilliance	lustro
brilliant	brillante
brisk, animated	animato
broken, arpeggiated	arpeggiando, arpeggiato

FRENCH	GERMAN
auteur	Textverfasser
mesure, tempo	Takt
numéro de la mesure	Taktzahl
barre	Taktstrich
baguette	Taktstock
barre transversale	Notenbalken
battement	Schlag, Schwebung
battre la mesure	Taktschlagen
commencement	Anfang, Eintretend
mélanger	mischen
audacieux, hardi	kühn, keck
emprunt	Entlehnung
sautillé	Springbogen
jouer avec l'archet	streichen
bravoure, courage	bravour, beherzt
arrêter	abbrechen
souffle	Atem
respiration	Luftpause
murmuré	hauchig
chevalet	Steg
éclat	Glanz
brillant	brillant, glänzend
animé	belebt
arpégé	arpeggiert, gebrochen

ENGLISH	ITALIAN
brusquely, abruptly	brusco, bruscamente
cadence, close	cadenza, chiusa
cadencing	cadenzale
caesura, cut	cesura
calm, calmly	calmato, calmando
calming	calmando
capricious	capriccioso
carelessly, with indifference	negligente
caressing, flattering	carezzando
chamber sonata	sonata da camera
characteristic, feature	caratteristica
chord	accordo
chorus, choir	coro
chorus, refrain	ritornello
church sonata	sonata da chiesa
clear, distinct	chiaro, nettamente
clef	chiave
coach (to)	provare
coda	coda
collection	raccolta
comfortable, leisurely	comodo
comical	buffo
composition	composizione
conduct (to)	dirigere

FRENCH	*GERMAN*
brusque, brusquement	barsch, heftig
cadence, terminaison	Schluss, Endung
cadentiel	kadenzierend
césure	Einschnitt
tranquille, calme	gelassen, beruhigend
calmant	beruhingend
capricieux	launenhaft
insouciant	gleichgültigkeit
caressant	kosend, schmeichelnd
sonata de chambre	Kammersonate
caractéristque	Merkmal
accord	akkord
choeur	Chor
refrain	Wiederholung, Refrain
sonate d'église	Kirchensonata
net, clair	deutlich, klar
clef, clé	Schlüssel
entrainer	korrepetieren
coda	Abschluss
collection	Sammlung
commodément	gemächlich,
comique	komisch
composition	Tonsatz
diriger	dirigieren

ENGLISH	*ITALIAN*
connoisseur	intenditore
consoling	consolante
continue [without break]	segue
contrary motion	moto contrario
count (to)	contare
counter-melody	controcanto
counterpoint	contrappunto
countersubject	controsoggetto
courtly	cortigianesco
create (to)	creare
cue	chiamata
cue, entry	entrée
cut	taglio
cycle, circle	ciclo
dancing	di danza
declamation, recitative	declamazione
decrease (to) [dynamics]	diminuire
deep, low	basso, grave
depress (to)	abbassare
descend, lower	descendere, abbassare
desperately	disperato
detached	staccato
determined	risoluto
development [thematic]	sviluppo, svolgimento

FRENCH	GERMAN
connaisseur	Kenner
consolant	tröstend
suivre, enchaînez	folgen
mouvement contraire	Gegenbewegung
compter	zählnen
contre-thème	Gegenmelodie
contrepoint	Kontrapunkt
contre-sujet	Gegensatz
de cour	höfisch
créer	schaffen
réplique	Stichwort
empressé, hâter	Einsatz
coupure	Streichung
cycle	Kreis
dansant	tänzerisch
déclamation	Deklamation, Rezitativ
diminuer	abschwellen
bas, profund	tief
abaisser	niederdrücken
descendre, abaisser	absteigen
désesperé	verzweifelt
détaché	abgestossen
décidé, décisif	gewiss
développement	Dürchführung

ENGLISH	ITALIAN
devoutedly	devoto
dexterity	abilità
diatonic	diatonico
diminish (to) [interval]	diminuire
dirge, funeral song	canto funebre
disc, recording	disco
discordant, out of tune	discordia
dissonance	dissonanza
distinct,clear	distinto, chiaro
divertisement	divertimento
divided	divisi
dot, dotted	punto, puntato
double tonguing	doppio colpo di lingua
doubled	doppio
down bow	arco in giu
downbeat	in battere
downward	discendente
draft, sketch	abbozzo
dragging	trascinando, stentando
dramatic	drammatico
dreamily	trasognato
dry	secco
dull [in tone]	sordo
duration, playing time	durata

FRENCH	*GERMAN*
pieusement	andächtig
dexterité	Fertigkeit
diatonique	diatonisch
diminuer	verkleinern, diminuieren
chant funèbre	Grabgesang, Todeslied
disque	Schallplatte
désaccordé	Diskordanz
dissonant	Dissonanz
nettement, distinctement	bestimmt, deutlich
divertissement	Divertimento
divisé	geteilt
point, pointé	Punkt, punktiert
double articulation	Doppelzunge
double	doppelt
tiré	Herstrich
frappé	abtaktig
descendant	abwärts
détente	Entwurf
traînant	schleppend
dramatique	dramatisch
comme dans un songe	traümerisch
sec, séche	kurz, trocken
sourd	kurzatmig
duré	Laufzeit

ENGLISH	*ITALIAN*
dying away, getting softer	dimenuendo, scemando
dying away	morendo, mancando
dying away	sperdendosi (perdendosi)
ear	orecchio
easygoing	disinvolto
echo, resonance	risonanza
eighth-note	croma
eleventh	undicesima
embouchure	imboccatura
emphatically	enfatico
encore, again	bis
end	fine
enharmonic	enarmonico
enthusiasm	entusiasmo
epilogue	postludio
episode	episodio
euphonious	eufonico
even, equalgend	equabile, uniforme
exact	giusto
excited, stirred	concitato
exercise (to)	esercitare
exhale	espirare
expand, extend	allargare

FRENCH	GERMAN
diminuendo, en diminuant	abnehmend, leiser werdend
diminuant, éteindre	verlöschend, hinsterbend, ersterbend
en mourant	verhallend
oreille	Ohr
alerte	ungezwungen
résonance	Nachklingen
croche	Achtelnote
onziàme	Undezime
embouchure	Ansatz, Mondloch
emphatique	nachdrücklich
encore	Zugabe
fin	Ende
enharmonique	enharmonisch
enthousiasme	Enthusiasmus
postlude	Nachspiel
couplet	Couplet
euphonie	Wohlklingend
égal	gleichmässig
précis, exact	genau
excité, animé	agitirt, erregt
exercise	üben
expirer	ausatmen
élargir	erweitern

ENGLISH	ITALIAN
expressively	espressivo
extol, praise	esaltare
fade out, die away	smorzarsi
fading away	estinguendo, mancando
fairly	mezzo
false	falsa
falsetto [voice]	falsetto
fantasia	fantasia
fast	presto
fauxbourdon	falso bordone
fee	onorario
feeble	fiacca, debole
felt	feltro
ferocious, wild	feroce
fervently	fervido
fiery	acceso, focoso
fifth [interval]	quinta
figure	cifra
fingering	diteggiatura
firmly	fermo
first violin	primo violino
flat [sign]	bemolle
floating	flottuante
flourish, fanfare	fanfara

FRENCH	*GERMAN*
expressivo	ausdrucksvoll
célébrer	erhaben
s'évanouir	abklingen
diminuant, éteindre	verlöschend
assez	ziemlich
faux	falsch
fausset	Falsett
fantaisie	Fantasie
vite, rapide	schnell
faux-bourdon	Fauxbourdon
cachet	Gage
faible	schwach
feutre	Filz
féroce, sauvage	wild
ardemment	inbrünstig
acceso, avec fougue	feurig
quinte	Quint
chiffrage	Ziffer
doigté	Fingersatz
ferme	fest
premier violon	Primgeige
bémol	Erniedrigunszeichen
flottant	flottant
fanfare, sonnerie	Tusch

ENGLISH	*ITALIAN*
flowing, fluid	scorrendo, scorrevole
flutter-tonguing	frullato
force, push [the sound]	forzare, rinforzare
forced, accented	sforzando, sforzato
fourth [interval]	quarta
free	libero
freely	a libito, beneplacito
frequency	frequenza
freshly	fresco
frivolous	frivolo
full [as in full voice]	pièno
full of feeling	molto sentimento (con)
gallop	galop, galoppo
gently, suavely	soave
glad, joyous	lieto
glissando, sliding	glissando
gloomy, dismal	tetro, cupo
gracefully	grazioso
grand, great	maestoso
grief, sadness	addolorato
grow louder	addensare, ispessire
gypsy	zingaro
hammered	martellato

FRENCH	GERMAN
coulant, facile	fliessend
articulation double	Flatterzunge
forcer	forcieren
renforçant	starken akzentuiertem
quarte	Quart
libre	frei
à volanté	ad libitum, belieben
fréquence	Frequenz
fraichement	frisch
frivole	frivol
plein, pleine	volltsnig, rund
beaucoup de sentiment (avec)	gefühlvoll
galop	Galopp
doucement	sanft
aisé	froh
glissando, en glissant	gleitend
sombre, triste	düster
aimable, gracieux	anmuthig, graziös
grand	grossartig
douleur, douloureaux	betrübt, schmerz
augmenter	anschwellen
tsigane	Zigeuner
martelé	hämmernd

ENGLISH	*ITALIAN*
hard	riverberante
harmonious	armonioso
harmony, setting, style	stile, scrittura
harshly	aspramente
harshness	durezza, asprezza
hastening, pressing	sollecitando
hear (to)	udire, ascoltare
heartfelt	sentito
held back	ritenuto
heroic	eroico
hesitate (to), retard (to)	ritardare
high	alto, acuto
hold, fermata, pause	fermata, corona
holding back	cedendo
hop, leap (to)	saltellare
hot, fiery, impetuous	di fuoco
hum (to)	brontolare
humming [with closed mouth]	bocca chiusa
humor	umore
hymn [of praise]	inno
imitation	imitazione

FRENCH	GERMAN
dur	schallhart
sonore	klangvoll
style, écriture	Satzart
aigrement, âpre	rauh, hart-klingend
dureté	Härte
empressé, hâter	eilen, hastig, triebend
entendre, écouter	hören
intime	innig
retenu	ritenuto
héroique	heroisch
hésiter	zögern
haut, aigu	hoch
point d'orgue, pause, fermata	Halt, Fermate
en cédent	nachgebend
sauter	höpsen
fougueux	hitzig
bourdonner	brummen
bouche fermé	brummstimmen
plaisant	launig
chanson laudative	Lobegesang
imitation	Nachahmung

ENGLISH	ITALIAN
impatiently	impazientemente
imperfect	imperfetto
impetuous	impetuoso
impetus, outburst	slancio
imposing in style	imponente
improvise (to)	improvvisare
in tempo	a tempo
inaudible	inudibile
incoherent, unconnected	incoerente
incomplete	incompleto
indication	indicato
inflection	inflessione
inhale (to)	inspirare
inspiration, enthusiasm	ispirazione
instruction, lesson	istruzione
intabulation	intavolatura
intensify (to)	intensificare
interpolate (to)	interpolare
interpretation	interpretazione
intonation	intonazione
intone (to)	intonare
inversion	rivolto
inverted mordent	mordente superiore
ironical	ironico

FRENCH	GERMAN
impatiemment	ungeduldig
imparfait	imperfekt
précipité	heftig, stürmish
impulsion, vitesse	impuls, Stosskraft,
imposant	imponierend
improviser	fantasieren
en measure	im Tact, im Zeitmas
inaudible	unhörbar
incohérent	unzusammen-hüngend
incomplet	unvollständig
indicatif	Andeutung
inflexion	Stimmfall
respirer	einatmen
inspiration, enthousiasme	begeisterung
enseignement	Unterricht
tablature	Intabulierung
intensifier	steigern
insérer	einschieben
interprétation	Vortrag
intonation	Intonation
entonner	intonieren
inversion	Umkehrung
pincé	Schneller, Preller
ironiquement	ironisch

ENGLISH	*ITALIAN*
joking	scherzando
joyous	gioioso
jubilant	giubbilose
key, mode, tonality	tono
keyboard	tastiera
lag behind (to)	restare indietro
lamenting	gemendo
languidly	languido
languishing	languendo
last, ultimate	ultimo
leaned upon	poggiato
leap, skip	taglio
ledger line	taglio linea supplementare
lightly	leggiero
line [of a staff]	linea
listen (to)	ascoltare
little by little, gradually	poco a poco
lively	vivo
long note	nota tenuta
loud, strong	forte
louder gradually	crescendo
lower, flatten	abbassare, bemollizzare
macabre	macabro
madly, frenetically	frenetico

FRENCH	GERMAN
badinant	scherzhaft
joyeux, gai	fröhlich, lebhaft
jubilant	jubelnd
tonalité	Tonart
clavier	Klaviatur
retarder	nachhinken
plaintif	gemendo
languissant	schmachtend
langueur	müde, erschlaffen
dernier	endlich
appuyer	aufhalten
saut	Sprung
ligne supplémentaire	Hilfslinie
facile	leicht
ligne	Linie
écouter	zuhören
peu a peu, graduellement	allmählich, gradweisse
vivement	lebendig, lebhaft
note tenue	Pfundnote
forte, à haut voix	forte, laut
crescendo	lauter werdend
baisser	erniedrigen
macabre	schauerlich
frénetique	frenetico, rasend

ENGLISH	*ITALIAN*
magnificent	magnifico
majestically	maestoso
manuscript paper	carta da musica
march	marcia
mark, sign	segno
marked, accented	marcato
martial	marziale
Mass for the dead	requiem
masterly, virtuoso	virtuoso
mellow	morbido
melodiously, singing	cantabile, cantando
melodrama	melodramma
melody	melodia
merrily, cheerful	gioioso
merry, festive	festoso, festivo
meter	tempo
mighty, powerful	possènte, potente
military	militare
minor [mode]	minore
minstrel	menestrello
mirror fugue	fuga a specchio
moderately, restrained	moderato
modulation	modulazione
mood	stato d'animo

FRENCH	GERMAN
magnifique	magnifico, prächtig
majestueux	majestätisch
papier à musique	Notenpapier
marche	Marsch
signe	Zeichen
marqué	markiert
martial	kriegerisch
Requiem, messe funèbre	Totenmesse
virtuose	virtuos
doux	weich
chantant	gesanglich, singend
mélodrame	Melodram
mélodie	Melodik
plaisant, joyeux	jovialisch
festivo	festlich, freudig
temps	Zeitmass
puissant, fort	mächtig
militaire	militärisch
mineur	Moll
ménestrel	Spielmann
fugue en miroir	Spiegelfuge
modéré	mässig, gehend
modulation	Modulation
climat	Stimmung

ENGLISH	*ITALIAN*
mordant [ornament]	mordente
more	più
motet	motetto
motion, movement	moto
motive	motivo
mournful, plaintive	flebile
movement [of a work]	movimento
moving, animated	mosso
muffled [voice]	scurito
music, tonal art	musica
music stand	leggio
mute	sordino
mysteriously	misterioso
narrator	testo
nervous, restless	irrequieto
nimble, agile	snèllo
ninth [interval]	nona
noble, grand	nobile
nocturne	notturno
noise	rumore
noisy	strepitoso
non-tonal	non tonale
nonet	nonetto
note, key	tasto

FRENCH	*GERMAN*
mordant	Mordent
plus	mehr
motet	Motette
mouvement	Bewegung
motif	Motiv
plaintif, triste	klagend
mouvement	Satz
mosso	bewegt
couvert, voilé	gedeckt
musique	Tonkunst
pupitre	Notenpult, Notenständer
sourdine	Dämpfer
mystérieusement	geheimnisvoll
récitant	Testo
inquiet, agité	unruhig, heftig bewegt
légér, agilement	hurtig, leicht
neuvième	None
noblement	edel
nocturne	Abendlied, Nocturne
bruit	Geräusch
bruyant	lärmend
atonal	nichttonal
nonet	Nonett
touche	Taste

ENGLISH	ITALIAN
note value	valore della note
obligatory	obbligato
oblique motion	moto obliquo
obsequies	esequies
octet	ottetto
of	di
or	ossia
orchestrate (to)	strumentare
origin, source	fonte
ornament (to), embellish (to)	figurare
ornaments	abbellimenti
out of tune	scordato
overtone	armonico
overture, prelude	preludio
paraphrase	parafrasi
passionately	appassionato
pastoral	pastorale
pathetic	patètico
pattern, model	modello
penetrating, shrill	pentrante, acuto
percussion section	batteria
perfect [interval]	giusto
perfect fifths (in)	quinte giuste

FRENCH	GERMAN
valeur de la note	Notenwert
obligé	obligat
mouvement oblique	Seitenbewegung
obsèques	Exequien
octuor	Oktett
de	auf
ou	oder
instrumenter	instrumentieren
source	Quelle
orner, figurer	figurieren
ornements	Manieren
désaccordé	verstimmt
harmonique	Oberton
ouverture	Vorspiel
paraphrase	Umspielung
passionné	leidenschaftlich
pastorale	Pastorale, Hirtenlied
pathétique	pathetisch
modèle	Modell, Vorlage
pénétrant	durchdringend
batterie	Batterie
juste, parfait	rein
quintes justes	quintenrein

ENGLISH	*ITALIAN*
perform (to)	rappresentare
performance	esecuzione
period [form]	frase, periodo
phrasing	articolazione
pitch, pitch level	altezza del suono
pity, mercy	pieta, pietoso
placid	pacato
play (to)	suonare
pleasing	piacevole, gradito
pluck (to)	pizzicare, strappare
plucked	pizzicato
podium, rostrum	podio
poet, lyricist	poeta
polite, graceful	garbato
polonaise	polacca
polythematic	politematico
pompous	pomposo
preparation	preparazione
print, edition	stampa
producer, artistic director	regista
production, stage direction	regia
progression	seguito
prompter	suggeritore
proudly, fiercely	fiero, fieramente

FRENCH	GERMAN
représenter	aufführen
exécution	Ausführung
période, partie	Periode
phrasé	Phrasieruing
hauteur du son	Tonhöhe
dolent	Mitleid
placide	ruhig, sanft
jouer	spielen
plaisant, charmant	gefällig, angenehm,
pincer	zupfen, anreissen
pincé	gezupft
podium	Podium
parolier, poète	Textdichter
gracieux	zierlich
polanaise	Polonaise
polythématique	vielthemig
pompeux	pompös
préparation	Vorbereitung
impression	Druck
régisseur	Spielleiter
régie	Regie
séquence	Folge
souffleur	Souffleur
fier, fièrement	fier, stolz

ENGLISH	*ITALIAN*
psalm	salmo
publisher	editore
quadruplet	quartina
quartet	quartetto
quicken	ravvivando
quickening, urging on	stringendo
quintet	quintetto
quintuplet	quintina
quote (to)	citare
raise (to), sharpen	alzare
range	estensione
range, compass	estensione
range [vocal]	estensione vocale
rapidly	rapidissimo
recitative	recitativo
recite (to)	recitare
record (to)	registrare
recording	registrazione
recur (to), return (to)	ricorrere
reduced, arranged	ridotto
reed	ancia
regulate	regolare
rehearsal	prova
reinforced, strengthened	rinforzato

FRENCH	*GERMAN*
psaume	Psalm
éditeur	Verleger
quartolet	Quartole
quatuor	Quartett
pressant	beschleunigung
pressant	drängend
quintette	Quintett
quintolet	Quintole
citer	zitieren
hausser	erhöhen
ambitus	Raum
ambitus	Umfang
registre	Stimmumfang
rapidement	rasch
récitatif	Rezitativ
réciter	rezitieren
enregistrer	einspielen
enregistrement	Aufnahme
revenir	wiederkehren
réduire	reduzieren
anche	Rohrblatt
régler	regulieren
répétition	Probe
renforcé	verstärkt

ENGLISH	*ITALIAN*
reintepretation	reinterpretazione
relax (to)	distendire
release (to)	abbandonare
remote	lontano
repeat from the beginning	da capo, dal segno
repeat sign	segni di ripetizione
reprint	ristampa
resolutely, decisively	deciso, decisamente
resolve (to)	risolvere
resonant	risonante
rest	pausa
restless, uneasy	inquietante
retrograde, crabwise	retrogrado
reverberation	riverberazione
review, criticize (to)	recensire
revise (to)	rivedare
rework (to), revise (to)	rielaborare
rhythm	ritmo
ricercare	ricercare
robbed rhythm	rubato
roguishly	malignamente
rounded, rich	ampio
rushing	volante
rustic, country-like	contadinesco

FRENCH	GERMAN
équivoque	Umdeutung
détendre	entspannen
lácher	loslassen
éloigné	entfernt
depuis le commencement	Anfang (von)
signe de reprise	Wiederholungszeichen
reproduction	Nachdruck
décidé, avec résolution	bestimmt, entschieden
résoudre	auflösen
résonnant	resonanzföhig
silence, pause	Pause
inquiet, agité	ruhelos, unheimlich
rétrograde	krebsgängig
réverbération	Nachhall
recenser	rezensieren
réviser	revidieren
retoucher	überarbeiten
rythme	Rhythmus
ricercar	Ricercar
rubato	rubato
espièglement	schalkhaft
rond, plein	rund
volant	fliegend
villageois	bauernlich

ENGLISH	*ITALIAN*
sad, mournful	mesto, triste
sad, painful	doloroso
scale	scala
scan	scandire
scenario	copione
score	partitura, spartito
section, part	sezione, parte
secular	profano
semitone, half tone	semitono
separate (to), articulate (to)	articolare
septet	settimino
sequence	sequenza
serenade	serenata
serious	serioso
sextet	sestetto
sextuplet	sestina
shake (to)	scuotere, agitere
sharp, shrill	stridento, strillo
shift [position]	smanicare
short score	particella
sibilant	sibilante
sigh	sospiro
signature	segnatura
similar, in a like manner	simile

FRENCH	GERMAN
douloureaux, triste	traurig, wehmütig
douloureaux	schmerzlich
gamme, échelle	Tonleiter
scander	skandieren
scénario	Drehbuch, Szenarium
partition	Partitur, Sparte
section, partie	Teil
profane	weltlich
demi-ton	Halbton
articuler	absetzen
septuor	Septett
séquence	Sequenz
sérénade	Stándchen
sérieux	ernst
sextuor	Sextett
sextolet	Sextole
secouer, agiter	schütteln
strident	schreiend
démancher	demanchieren
partie	Particell
lettre sifflante	Zischlaut
soupir	Seufzer
signature	Signatur
similaire	ebenfalls

ENGLISH	ITALIAN
simply	semplice
sing with (to)	cantare insieme
singer, vocalist	cantante
sixteenth-note	semicroma
sixth [interval]	sesta
slow	tardo, tardamento
slow but not too much	largo ma non troppo
slow down (to)	rallentare
slowing down	ritardando, raffrenando, rallentando
slur	legatura
slurred, tied	legato
sobbing	singhiozzando
soft [dynamics]	piano
soft [texture]	assorbente
softer, gradually	decrescendo
solemn, heavy, slow	grave, pesante
solemnly	solenne
solfeggio	solfeggio
sonata	sonata
song	canzone
soon, quick	tosto
sorrowful, pathetic	dolente, dolore
sound (to)	suonare

FRENCH	GERMAN
simplement	einfach
chanter avec	mitsingen
chanteur	Sänger
double croche	Sechzehntelnote
sixte	Sexte
lent	langsam
mais pas trop lent	mässig langsam
ralentir	nachlassen
ralentissant, étendre	zurückhaltend, langsamer werdend
ligature	Bindeklappe
lié	gebunden
pleurant	schluchzend
doux	leise
mou	schallweich
en diminuant	leiser werdend
lent, avec gravité	schwer
solennel	feierlich
solfège	Solfeggio
sonate	Sonate
mélodie	Lied
bientôt, vite	bald, schnell
dolent, triste	schmerzhaft
sonner	erklingen

ENGLISH	*ITALIAN*
soundproof	isolante
spacing [of a chord]	posizione
sparkling	scintillante
speaking	parlando, parlante
species	specie
speech-song, inflected speech	canto-parlato
spirited, resolutely	animoso, animosamente
spiritual, sacred	spirituale
splice (to)	congiungere
square notation	notazione quadrata
staff, stave	pentagramma
standard pitch	diapason
stanza	strofa
stem [of a note]	gambo della note
step	grado
stepwise	congiunto, di grado
stop	arresto
stopped [horn]	chiuso
strengthening	rinforzando
stress	enfasi
stretto	stretto
strict time, measured	misurato, a battuta
strict	severo, rigoroso

FRENCH	*GERMAN*
insonorisé	schalldicht
position	Lage
brillant	funkelnd
parler	redend, sprechen
espèce	Gattung
sprechgesang	Sprechgesang
animé, hardiment	animoso, beherzt
spirituel	geistlich
coller	kleben
notation carée	Quadratnotation
portée	Liniensystem
diapason standard	Normalton
strophe	Strophe
queue de la note	Notenhals
degré	Schritt
par degrés conjoints	schrittweise
arrêt, silence	Stillstand
étouffé	gestopft
renforcent	stärker werdend
accent	Schwerpunkt
strette	Engführung
mesure, à la mesure	abgemessen
sévère	streng

ENGLISH	ITALIAN
string	corda
structure	struttura
strum (to)	strimpellare
strumming	strimpello
stylishly	gusto [con]
subject, theme	soggetto
successively	successivamente
suddenly	subito
support (to)	sostenare
suspension	ritardo
sustained	sostenuto, tenendo
sustaining pedal	prolungamento
swaying	barcollante
sweetly, softly	dolce, raddolcendo
syllabic	sillabico
syllabic notation	notazione sillabica
syllable	sillaba
sympathetic	simpatico
symphony	sinfonia
syncopation	sincope
tablature	tablatura
tail, flag [of a note]	codetta
tempestuous	tempestoso
tenor	tenore

FRENCH	GERMAN
corde	Saite
structure	Struktur
tapoter	klimpern
tapotage	Geklimper
goét [avec]	geschmackvoll
sujet	Thema
successivement	hintereinander
subitement	plötzlich, sofort
soutenir	stützen
retard	Vorhalt
tenu, soutenu	gehalten, getragen
prolongement	Tastenfessel
oscillant	schwankend
doucement, doux	zart, süss
syllabique	syllabisch
notation syllabique	Tonsilbenschrift
syllabe	Silbe
sympathetique	mitklingend
symphonie	Symphonie
syncope	Synkopierung
tablature	Griffnotation
crochet de la note	Notenfahne
orageux	stürmisch
ténor	Tenor

ENGLISH	*ITALIAN*
tense, rigid, taut	rigido, teso
tension	tensione
thematic	tematico
theoretical	teorico, teoretico
thin, reedy	esile
third	terza
thread	filo
threateningly	minacciosamente
tie	tenuto
time signature	segno d'indicazione
timidly	pauroso
tinkle (to)	tintinnare
tip, point	punta
title page	frontespizio
to	al
to take off [remove]	levare
tonal	tonale
tonality	tonalità
tone, sound	suono
tone color	timbro
tonic	tonica
touch	tocco
transcription	trascripzione
transition	passaggio

FRENCH	GERMAN
rigide, tendu	straff
tension	Spannung
thématique	thematisch
théorique	theoretisch
fin	dünn
tierce	Terz
fil	Garn
minacciosamente	bedrohlich, drohend
tenue	Bindung
signe de la mesure	Taktvorzeichen
craintif, timide	angstvoll
tinter	bimmeln
pointe	Spitze
page de titre	Titelblatt
à	bis
éloigner	wegschaffen
tonal	tonlich
tonalité	Tonalität
son	Klang, Schall
timbre	Tonfarbe
tonique	Tonika
attaque	Spielart
transcription	übertragung
passage	Durchgang

ENGLISH	ITALIAN
transpose (to)	traspotare
trembling	tremolando
tremendous	tremendo
tremolo	tremolo
triad	triade
trill, shake	trillo
trill (to), warble (to)	cantarellare
trio	terzetto
triplet	terzina
tune (to)	accordare
tune, melody	melodia
turn [the page!]	volti!
turntable	piatto portadischi
two voices or instruments	a due
unaccented	non accentato
unconnected, non legato	scucito
undecided [in style]	irresoluto
understudy	sostituto
undulating, wavering	ondeggiando
unhurried	deliberatamente
unison	unisono
unprepared	non preparato
up bow	arco in su
upbeat	anacrusi

FRENCH	GERMAN
transposer	transponieren
tremblant	zitternd
terrible	enorm, riesig
trémolo	Tremolo
triade	Dreiklang
trille	Triller
fredonner	trällern
trio	Terzett
triolet	Triole
accorder	einstimmen
air	Weise, Melodik
tournez [la page!]	umblättern!
plateau	Plattenteller
à deux	zwei Gesang
non accentué	unbetonnt
détaché	abgezetzt
indécis	unentschieden
doublure	Ersatzspieler
ondoyant	wogend
régulié	bedächtig
unisson	Einklang, Prim
non préparé	unvorbereitet
poussé	Hinstrich
anacrouse	Auftakt

ENGLISH	ITALIAN
upper notes, treble	altezza
urgently	insistamente
vague	vago
veiled, husky [voice]	velato
velocity	scorrevolezza
velvety	vellutato
version	versione
verve	brio
very	assai
vibrate (to)	vibrare
vibrato	vibrato
virtuosity	virtuosità
vocal inflection, speech-melody	inflessione della voce
vocal ornaments	abbellimenti vocali
vocalise	vocalizzo
voice, part	parte, voce
walking , moderately	andante
waver in pitch, sing off pitch	stonare
weak [voice]	sommesso
weaken	indebolendo
whispering, murmuring	mormorando
whistle (to)	fischiare
whole note	semibrevis

FRENCH	GERMAN
hauteur	Höhe
insistence [avec]	inständig
vague	unbestimmt
voilé, brumeux	verschliert
vèlocitè	Geläufigkeit
velouté	samtig
version	Fassung
verve, élan	Schmiss
beaucoup, très	sehr
vibrer	schwingen, vibrieren
vibrato	Bebung
virtuosité	Kunstfertigkeit
inflexion de la voix	Sprechmelodie
broderies	Singmanieren
vocalise	Vocalise
voix, partie	Stimme
andante, allant	andante, gehend
détonner	detonieren
voilé	demütig
affaiblissant	schwächer
murmuré	murmelnd, gehaucht
siffler	pfeifen
semi-brève	Semibrevis, Ganze

ENGLISH	ITALIAN
whole tone	tono [intero]
with	con, col, colla
without	senza
wobble (to)	tremolare
zeal	zelo

FRENCH	GERMAN
ton entier	Ganzton
avec	mit
sans	ohne
chevroter	wackeln
zèle	zele, eifger